Social Thinking® and Me

Kids' Guidebook to Social Emotional Learning
Book 1

By

Michelle Garcia Winner and Linda K. Murphy

Social Thinking Publishing, Santa Clara, California

www.socialthinking.com

Social Thinking® and Me
Kids' Guidebook to Social Emotional Learning

Michelle Garcia Winner and Linda K. Murphy

ISBN: 978-1-936943-22-7

Think Social Publishing, Inc.
404 Saratoga Avenue, Suite 200
Santa Clara, CA 95050
Tel: (408) 557-8595
Fax: (408) 557-8594

Illustrations by NewWaySolutions, Santa Fe, Argentina
This book was printed and bound in the United States by Mighty Color Printing.

TSP is a sole source provider of Social Thinking products in the U.S.
Books may be purchased online at www.socialthinking.com

DedicaTion

For all the students who help us be better teachers and people,
this book is for you! You make us smile, laugh and learn every day.

ConTenTS

Introduction

Being "social" – what's that all about? When you were younger, it was probably mostly about playing games with other kids, or getting along with your brother or sister. You probably heard your parents tell you to do one thing or another when you were around other people, like:

"Be nice to your sister."
"Don't forget to ask your grandmother about her vacation."
"Even if you don't like the gift, be sure to say thank you anyways... and smile."
"Pay attention! I'm talking to you!"

All of these comments are about how people expect other people to act in different situations. And that's a big part of what being social is all about – learning ways to be around others when you're in a group. (Hint: a group can be just two people!)

It would be nice if there were social rules we could all learn so we know exactly what to say or what to do in different social situations, wouldn't it? In fact, there are... Your teacher has probably told you about different rules that apply while you're in school. They're things like pay attention when an adult is talking, raise your hand to talk in class, listen when another classmate is talking, no hitting or fighting, no cheating on tests, etc. Your parents might have different rules for being at home: bedtime is 9 o'clock, Saturday is clean your room day, don't borrow things without asking, no electronics at the dinner table, and things like that.

But a lot of the time the social rules we use are "hidden." What does that mean? It means people don't talk about them very much, they're not usually taught, and they're not the type of facts you learn about in school. The hidden rules are kind of like guidelines that help you figure out how to be social in any situation. And here's another hint: they're a LOT about *thinking*... not just about your behavior. This thinking is called your "social thinking." It can help you with your behavior, so you have a better idea of what to say, or what to do (or not do) when you're with others.

That's what this book is all about: teaching you ways to be social so that whenever you're in a group, like a soccer team, a classroom, your family, or even just hanging out with friends at home, you can figure out what's expected for that situation. (Hint: different situations have different hidden rules!)

Sometimes social situations are complicated, and it may feel like it's impossible to figure out how to act in them. We all know that feeling! But the wise people who wrote this book are great at making something that can feel complicated easier for you to understand. They're experts at taking a big social idea or situation and breaking it apart into smaller pieces so you can learn about things one step at a time. That's great, right?

How to use *Social Thinking and Me* to help you the most

There are two books in this set. Book 1, the *Kids' Guidebook* (the one you're starting to read right now), will help you learn about the Social Thinking Vocabulary. Think

about when you first started learning about math. There were words that were unfamiliar to you, but once you learned them, they helped you make sense and better understand the rest of math. They became tools you could remember to use. You also learned different math rules and operations that would help you solve math problems. The Social Thinking Vocabulary is a lot like that. In each chapter of this book you'll learn different social terms and social strategies that will become the tools you use to solve social problems or figure out ways to act in a situation so everyone feels good about being together!

You'll be learning a LOT of great information from this book and for this reason we want you to know this book is not meant to be read all at once. It's a good idea to go through it the first time with a teacher or other adult, chapter by chapter. That way you can ask questions and the adult can explain things along the way to help you better understand the material. After you've gone through a chapter, you can read it again by yourself, as often as you'd like. This will help you get better and better at being social and learning how to be around others when you're in a group.

The second book, *Social Thinking and Me Thinksheets*, was created to give you lots of practice in learning about the Social Thinking Vocabulary. In it you'll find different exercises to complete that go with each chapter in the *Kids' Guidebook* you're working through. Some of the thinksheets are easier and some of them might be more challenging, so it's best to work through them with an adult also. (Hint: we call them *thinksheets* instead of *worksheets* because you'll be using your social brain to *think* about the different situations first before you do the "social math" to figure them out.) We all need to practice our social skills so we can get better and better at them over time!

Ready to get started? It's going to be a fun ride, learning about your social brain, your thoughts and feelings, about those hidden rules we mentioned, and what's expected (and unexpected!) to do or say in different social situations! Being social can feel confusing, frustrating, and complicated at times; we know that. This *Kids' Guidebook* is going to *guide you through it* in a way that's meant just for you to understand. The more you learn the better you'll get at being a good social partner, a good social detective (we'll explain that in the book!), and a solver of social problems. The skills you learn through this book will help you in all your coming years.

"Each mistake teaches you something new about yourself.
There is no failure, remember, except in no longer trying.
It is the courage to continue that counts."
— Chris Bradford, *The Way of the Sword*

CHAPTER 1

WhaT Is SociaL Thinking?

Our brains are preTTy much responsibLe for everything we do, say, and think about! There are so many ways our brains think — and often our thinking leads to learning.

Some students like to think and learn about how computers work. Some students are more interested in thinking and learning about video games and how to get really good at them. Others might like to think and learn about whales, sporting events, or how trees grow. We think and learn about all sorts of different things.

It may be a surprise that you do a lot of learning beyond what your teacher is teaching!

There are other types of thinking and learning that your brain has been quietly trying to do since you were born. This is described as something your brain does "quietly" because the learning happens without you even really noticing it! For example, you learned to say words and then to speak in sentences. By now you're learning to use your language in all types of ways. But you probably never noticed that you're getting better at communicating every month you live!

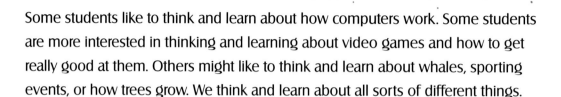

Learning To Talk To others is just one part of communicating. Another part of communicating is with your body. You probably point to something, like a drink, to let your mom know you want some. You might turn away from someone when you're mad.

That's what we call **nonverbal communicating.** It sends a silent message to others!

The Type of Thinking your brain is doing To figure ouT yourseLf and oTher peopLe is whaT we caLL SociaL Thinking. When you use your social thinking, you think about what others are trying to do or tell you. You also use social thinking to think about what you can do to let people know what you want or how you feel. And you do this in a way that helps others feel comfortable. It's a lot to think about!

You can start by trying to notice your own social thinking. When you're in your classroom, watch your teacher and think about what you see. A lot of the time you can figure out her plan by noticing her body language. This means noticing things like where are her eyes looking? What are her arms and hands doing? What's her facial expression? If you can notice some part or all of these things, you're already using the social thinking part of your brain.

The more you think about these things, the more you're learning how to be with people. This is why it's called social learning. Social learning isn't just about thinking though. It also means figuring out what to do once you think about how to be with different people in different situations. (A situation is what's happening at a specific place and time. It includes the people who are involved in what's happening.)

Being a good SociaL Thinker Takes pracTice. We don't get it right all the time. That's okay — we can learn as we go along.

Think about what to do if you want to tell your mom you're hungry. You're first supposed to think about her by looking with your eyes to see where she is and what she's doing. Once you figure out what she's doing, you figure out if this is a good time to tell her you're hungry. What if you're with your mom at home and you see she's talking on the phone and she looks pretty serious? Most kids in this situation would think about what they see. They would make a smart guess to figure out this isn't the time

This boy is not using his social thinking.

to interrupt their mom to say they're hungry. A good social thinker would know you should wait until she's off the phone before asking her to help get a snack.

Remember how thinking leads to learning, and the more you learn to think about things the more things you learn? Most four- and five-year-old kids will not stop to think about what their mom is doing before they tell her they're hungry. That's because kids who are four or five haven't learned to become a good social thinker yet! Every year you learn more about social thinking and how to do things in bigger and better ways. This is called **getting more mature**. Another fun way to describe this is we're developing our "social smarts."

Some of the social things you learn happen without you noticing them too much. For instance, maybe you see another student get in trouble for texting during class.

This boy is using his social thinking.

You pretty much figure out from this that if you text, you'll get in trouble too! Watching what others do is one way to get better at social thinking. With some of the other social stuff, parents, teachers, or other adults can help guide you. Either way, the purpose of using your social thinking is to help you learn more about yourself and other people. That will help you figure out the best way to behave so people will want to include you in their group. It will also help you learn what you can say or do to make your teacher, parent, or principal feel good about you! And here's a little secret. Social thinking helps people figure out who we *do or don't* want to be with. For example, it helps us figure out which kids like the same things we like. It even helps us figure out which people we should probably avoid.

When you were really little, you started out by only talking to your family or other people who helped take care of you. But now you spend time around other kids your own age a lot of the time. It takes extra work to learn to be with other kids your age. You have to share things, work in a group, and pay attention to how they feel. You even need to figure out what's good to say or do when you're with them.

In this book, you'll learn more about your own social thinking. This will help you continue to become better (more mature) socially when you're with all people — and especially with kids your own age.

The purpose of using your social Thinking is To help you Learn more abouT yourseLf and oTher peopLe.

Now, go explore how all this information applies to you in the Thinksheets book.

Let's Recap Chapter 1
What Is Social Thinking?

● I'm working on becoming a social thinker. In fact, everyone is!

● This means I'm using my brain to think about other people when I'm with them.

● I'm also using my brain to think about the situation I may be in.

● I'm trying to figure out what other people might be thinking or feeling. That will help me figure out the best way to behave so others will want to be around me.

● It's okay to make mistakes while I develop my social smarts. Everyone makes mistakes.

● I can always ask my parents and teachers for help.

● Becoming a social thinker can be hard work, but I'll get better and better at it as I practice.

CHAPTER 2

Social Thinking = Flexible Thinking

Most of us understand that our bodies bend and that we can make a wire bend in different directions. When something bends really well, we call it "flexible." We often don't realize the thoughts in our brain can be flexible as well.

KEEP IN MIND:

When you use

flexible Thinking

you can figure

Things ouT!

When we Think in a flexible way, iT means we can sTay caLm and Try To figure ouT a SociaL SiTuaTion. Everyone has different thoughts and feelings and may look at a situation in different ways. We can look at the situation, think with our eyes, and find clues to help us do that. But what's interesting is that others may look at the same situation and figure out something different than we did. As we think in different ways about a situation and notice how others may think about that same situation (their "perspective"), we're being flexible.

Here are some specific ways that being flexible works.

When people say things that mean something different from what you thought they meant, you can figure it out.

🔵 If you hear someone say "take a seat," you might think it means you should pick up your chair and take it somewhere. But if you use your flexible thinking and think with your eyes, you'll notice that no one else is picking up a chair. Then you may remember (or learn) this phrase may also mean, "please sit down."

- If someone says, "You have to let someone else be first in line today," it means that someone else would like to have the experience of being first. It doesn't mean that person doesn't like you or that you're not a special person in the room. It just means the person in charge needs to think about what other people would like to do as well.

People can do Things That you may noT immediaTeLy underStand. If you use your flexible brain, you can better figure out what they mean by what they're doing.

- If someone knocks into your body while walking past you, it may not mean that person is being mean to you. If you think about it, you may realize that the halls are crowded. Sometimes bodies just collide because there's not enough room for everyone to share space without touching each other.

- If a teacher calls on somebody besides you to answer a question, even when your hand is raised, it's usually because she wants to give everyone a turn. She wants to call on different students in her class every day, each day of the week. When the teacher doesn't call on you, it's not because she doesn't care what you have to say. It's because she has a lot of students and she's interested in every one of them. She can't have them speak all at the same time because then it would just sound like noise!

You understand that you have to think about what other people want or need. Sometimes this is different from what you want!

Being flexible means you Try and figure out how To be with others without always wanting To get your own way!

If you can Learn To accept changes in your routine without getting upset, you're Learning To be flexible!

- If you refuse to go to any restaurant with your family but the one you like, you're not being flexible. This can be very hard on your family. Everyone likes to do things they like to do. But people often let others have choices to show these other people they're thinking about what they like to do as well. You're being flexible when you agree to do some things because you understand this makes others feel good. You're also being flexible when you're good at turn taking and letting other people choose where to go or what to do.

- If you won't stop using your tablet to get ready for bed, you're being inflexible. This can really upset your parents and siblings, especially if you start to yell or argue because you want to keep playing! Flexibility requires you to think about what's best for you (getting a good night's sleep) and those around you. When you stay calm, it makes others feel calm, which helps them feel good about you.

You may be used to things happening in a certain order. You like it when a schedule or routine is followed. However, sometimes our schedules and routines have interruptions in them. Mostly that's okay. If you can learn to accept changes in your routine without getting upset, you're learning to be flexible!

Being inflexible

Being flexible

Being flexible means you think about what's best for you AND those around you.

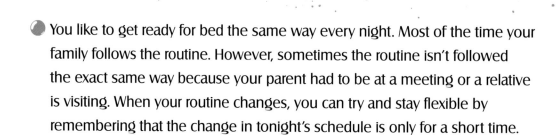

You like to get ready for bed the same way every night. Most of the time your family follows the routine. However, sometimes the routine isn't followed the exact same way because your parent had to be at a meeting or a relative is visiting. When your routine changes, you can try and stay flexible by remembering that the change in tonight's schedule is only for a short time. Things will probably return to normal tomorrow or soon.

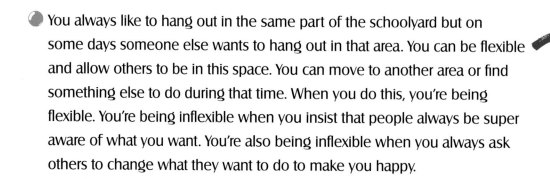

You always like to hang out in the same part of the schoolyard but on some days someone else wants to hang out in that area. You can be flexible and allow others to be in this space. You can move to another area or find something else to do during that time. When you do this, you're being flexible. You're being inflexible when you insist that people always be super aware of what you want. You're also being inflexible when you always ask others to change what they want to do to make you happy.

Learning to have flexible thoughts will help you stay calm and understand that other people also have things they need or want. When our thoughts are flexible, we can have flexible behaviors when we're around others, too. Being flexible means you can understand you don't get your way all the time. You understand we have to take turns so each of us gets our way at different times.

Being flexible also means you try to take a few extra moments to figure out what other people are doing. Or, you can try to figure out what they mean by what they say. When you think you already know or insist you should just get your way all the time, you're being inflexible!

Stuck thinking

Flexible thinking

Here are some other examples of situations where you can try to use your flexible thinking:

KEEP IN MIND:

Inflexible Thinking

= Stuck Thinking.

Stuck on your

own ideas.

- When your schedule or plans change unexpectedly at school or at home. For example, maybe you have to stay inside during lunchtime because it's raining, or maybe you can't go to the movies because your mom is sick. Being flexible also helps you match your reaction to the size of the problem better.

- When you don't know exactly what's going to happen next. For example, at the beginning of the school year everyone is getting used to the new routine. You may not always know what's coming next.

● When someone asks you to try something new, like a food, a game, or even a new way to play a game. One example is if another kid invites you to play chess and you're used to playing chess against the computer but not with another kid. Another is if your mom wants you to try a new food she thinks you'll like.

● When other kids want to play a different game than you want to play. For example, you want to play checkers but your friends want to play a card game.

● When other kids want to do a group project in a different way than you want to do it. For example, you think the group should use pictures from the Internet but the other kids want to make their own drawings. Or the other kids think the group should add a picture of a house, and you think it should be a castle.

● When your teacher asks you to do something different than what you're used to doing. For example, she asks you to sit at a different desk than the one you've been sitting at for the past month.

● When something you're used to doing happens unexpectedly in a different way. For example, you always bring your iPod to school and suddenly realize that today you forgot to bring it. Or your mom always packs pretzels in your lunch box and today she packed crackers.

● When you do something in a different order than you're used to doing it. For example, maybe your lunch table usually goes to get your food first in the cafeteria. This time a teacher asks your group to go second, third, or even last instead.

IT's expected that you try to be flexible when you're with other people. In fact, when you use flexible thinking, you're using a strategy that helps you be a person who thinks about others. Other people will feel comfortable and happy around you. They'll have good thoughts about you.

When we're flexible, our time with other people usually goes a lot more smoothly. This means we get done what we want to get done without having any arguments, and everyone feels good. When we're flexible, we're also more efficient with our time. This means we don't waste time on the little decisions that won't matter tomorrow or the next day. Instead, we use our time to be together in a calm and happy way. We focus on what we need and want to do as a team.

BEING A FLEXIBLE THINKER	
Flexible Thinking	**Stuck Thinking**
Thinking of Others Person	Just Me person
People feel good	People feel tense, frustrated, mad, or sad
We get things done	
Expected behavior	Situation is difficult, we don't get things done
	Unexpected behavior

When people aren't using flexible thinking, other people usually get upset because it seems like the inflexible persons aren't thinking about anyone but themselves. When people are only focused on what they want or need, it can make others feel upset, stressed, impatient, or frustrated. When people aren't flexible, it makes the situation difficult and frustrating for everyone. Instead of a smooth or enjoyable time together, there will be bumps, or disagreements, that don't feel good to anyone.

Being inflexible when you're with other people is unexpected behavior.
When someone isn't flexible, others may think that person is selfish or is a person who doesn't care about others. They'll probably have uncomfortable thoughts about that person.

Learning to be flexible is hard for everyone.
We have to try to think about other people and how our own behavior makes other people think or feel. That's a lot to think about! But it's important to learn to be a more flexible thinker. It's something we get better and better at over time and with practice.

Now, go explore how all this information applies to you in the Thinksheets book.

LeT's Recap ChaPTer 2
Social Thinking = Flexible Thinking

● When I think in a flexible way, it means I stay calm and try to figure out a social situation.

● Thinking in a flexible way is important for everyone, not just me! My family, friends, teachers, and other kids need to think in a flexible way too.

● I can think with my eyes to find the clues in a situation and consider the thoughts and feelings of the people around me.

● When I'm more flexible with my friends, teachers, and parents, it helps them feel happy, safe, and relaxed when I'm with them. When others have these good feelings because I'm flexible, they usually will have good thoughts about me.

● I like people having good thoughts about me, and I like to have good thoughts about other people too. When I think about it, I like it when people are flexible with how they treat me as well!

I'LL pracTice using fLexibLe Thinking!

CHAPTER 3

Social Thinking Vocabulary:
Words To Help You Think and Learn About Being With Others

In Teaching Social Thinking some special vocabulary words are used.
These words help you become a better social thinker in all sorts of different situations.
They help you think about what's happening at any moment, how you're thinking and
feeling, and how other people may be thinking and feeling.

KEEP IN MIND:

A good Social Thinker knows how To be wiTh oThers in a way ThaT's good for everyone.

What if you think you're already really good at social thinking? Well, there's always more to learn! Just like you can never learn all the words in the English language, you'll never know everything there is to know about social thinking. This is because as you get older, the thoughts and feelings you and your peers have change or "mature." The way you talk and act around others changes too. This means there are always new things to learn. But no matter how old you're today, one important thing stays the same. A good Social Thinker knows how To be wiTh oTher people in a way ThaT's good for everyone.

In this chapter you'll learn about the following Social Thinking Vocabulary and some other connected ideas that are important for your social learning:

- Thinking and Feeling
- Using Your Senses
- Thinking with Your Eyes
- Hidden Rules and the Situation
- Using Social Memory
- Making a Smart Guess

Some of these ideas have whole chapters devoted to them, because you'll use them a lot! It's a good idea to take your time with this chapter and not try to read it all at once.

Thinking and Feeling

There's a whole chapter in this book about how thinking and feeling are connected. But just to get you started, think about this. **You have ThoughTS and oTher peopLe have ThoughTS Too.** Sometimes they're the same and other times they can be different, even when you're both thinking about the same thing.

You think about the people around you or the people you like to remember. Other people think about you and people they like to remember. When you're at school, you think about the other kids in your class, even when you don't realize you're thinking about them. And they think about you. When you're in line at the movies, you have thoughts about the people around you. The other people in line may have thoughts about you. We have thoughts about people we see around us. We also have thoughts about people even when they're not around us! For example, you might like to think about your grandparents even when they're not around!

The weird Thing abouT ThoughTS is They're compLeTeLy inVisibLe, buT They can be Very powerfuL. Some thoughts we hardly notice and other thoughts can seem really big at times. Some thoughts we can pretty easily get out of our heads. With others we have to work hard to make them go away. It's this way for all of us.

What might these boys be thinking in each picture?

Your ThoughTS are connecTed To your feeLings. Feelings are physical sensations in our bodies that seem to pop up on their own. By your age most kids remember a good thought or something fun they did that made them feel happy. And most kids your age can remember things that made them feel mad, sad, or even scared. Sometimes people use the word emotions instead of the word "feelings." Feelings and emotions can mean pretty much the same thing, so don't get confused if you hear people use both words.

In this book you'll learn that our feelings are important clues to figure out more about our thinking. Before we get there, here's something important to think about. **When we're in a siTuaTion wiTh oThers, whaT we say or do isn'T onLy because of whaT we Think. IT's aLso based on how we feeL abouT The siTuaTion!** And the same is true for those around us. Other people have their own feelings and what we say or do creates feelings in them!

But, wait! How does all this information get into our brains to start with? One answer involves our senses. It's time to think about how some of our senses help us be better social thinkers.

Using Your Senses

In science class kids often learn that our senses send invisible signals to our brain about what's going on around us. You probably remember learning about your five senses when you were a little bit younger. Here they are for you to review:

- Seeing with your eyes

- Hearing with your ears

- Smelling with your nose

- Tasting with your tongue

- Touching with your skin

The senses aren't part of Social Thinking Vocabulary words — but they're still important for your social thinking! Think of them as messengers. You use them to get information into your social brain so it can think and process that information to help you figure out the situation.

Four of the senses help you with your social thinking. Can you guess which one does not? That's right - it's tasting. The others are important, though, so let's talk more about them.

Seeing/Eyes: Your eyes help you look around for social clues and cues. There's more on this coming up soon in this chapter.

Hearing/Ears: Your ears help you hear the words people are saying, their tone of voice, or other sounds around you.

Your senses feed information to your social brain to help you figure things out!

Smelling/Nose: You're probably wondering what your nose has to do with this. Your nose picks up different smells around you and sends that information to your brain. Your brain can use that "data" as another clue about what's going on. Just like hearing, sometimes your ability to smell helps you know what will happen next. For example, maybe you smell dinner cooking. This helps you make a smart guess that you'll have to stop what you're doing to go eat very soon.

Touching/Skin: When you touch something, your skin sends signals to your brain so you can feel the thing you're touching. Your brain tells you it's cold or hot, smooth or rough, hard or soft, or other things like that. Touch is one way of the nonverbal ways we communicate with others.

By themselves, our senses just "take in" the information and send it to our brain. It's our brain's job to think about and interpret all of the information to make sense of it. That's how our senses help with our social thinking.

Thinking with Your Eyes

Your eyes are very powerful! They can help you notice other people and what's happening in a situation. This is called **observing**. When people are good observers, they're gathering information to help them figure out what people are thinking and feeling. We call this being a SociaL deTecTive.

But your eyes have to partner up with your brain for things to make sense! We call this Thinking with your eyes. You may also hear people say "listen with your eyes" which means the same thing!

What can the boy figure out by thinking with his eyes?

This book talks a lot about **Thinking with your eyes** because it's pretty important. You'll find it again and again in many different chapters. It's a lot more than just looking at what's around you! Your job, starting right now, is to practice being a social detective to notice things and people around you. Good social thinkers are always thinking with their eyes!

KEEP IN MIND:

A situation contains clues, and your social detective skills help you find them!

Hidden Rules and the Situation

"Situation" is a word that covers all the things going on around you. When you're using your social thinking brain in a situation, you think about the *what*, the *where*, and the *who*.

- What's happening around me?

- Where is it happening? Am I at school, at home, at a special dinner in a fancy restaurant, etc.? The where is also called the "context" of the situation.

- Who's involved? Are these people familiar to me or strangers? Are they adults or kids?

When your teacher talks about the "setting" in a story, she's really asking you to think about the situation. A situation contains clues, and your social detective skills can help you find them.

For example, in the story of "Goldilocks and the Three Bears" the story setting is the bears' home. Goldilocks isn't friends with the bears but she goes into their home without them knowing it. She eats their food, breaks a chair, and messes up their beds. This is pretty upsetting to the bear family when they discover what happened. If Goldilocks was a relative coming to visit the bear family, like Baby Bear's aunt, that would have changed the situation and their feelings about it. It would have been okay if their aunt ate some food or messed up their bed. This is an example of how a situation and the people in it can affect people's thoughts and feelings.

Situations have **hidden rules** in them. These rules are called "hidden" because people don't talk about every little thing you need to do each time you're in a different situation. And, hidden rules can be different from one situation or setting to the next! For instance, it's not okay to talk in a loud voice during a movie at the theatre. But it's fine to use a loud voice when you're playing baseball outside with friends.

Some students have a harder time using their brain to figure out the hidden rules. All students, at one time or another, have a hard time with this. That's one reason why this book was written. **When you use your social deTecTive skiLLs and Think wiTh your eyes, you can noTice The cLues in a siTuaTion.** These clues can help you make a smart guess about the hidden rules of that situation. And once you have an idea of the hidden rules, you have an idea of what things you should and shouldn't do.

For example, imagine you get to school and you have a substitute teacher. Even though you're still in your same classroom, the person in charge is different. Students know the substitute teacher will probably run the class a little differently. This means students think with their eyes and listen with their ears to figure out the substitute teacher's hidden rules. If the teacher says it's time for math, even though your regular teacher does math after science, most kids figure out they should put away other things, take out their math book next, etc.

Here's another little bit of information no one may have ever told you. Having to figure out the hidden rules of a situation isn't just something you do when you're in class at school. You're expected to do this whenever you're around other people, even if you don't plan to talk to them! Examples are when you're at the movies, the mall, a church, or a birthday party.

You're also expected to figure out the hidden rules at home as well. Yes, there are even hidden rules in your own home. Here's one example: the closed bedroom door. When a family member has his or her bedroom door closed, the hidden rule is to knock and ask if you can come in before opening the door.

If you understand and follow the hidden rules in a situation, people around you will likely feel comfortable and even proud of you. This shows them you know how to work well as part of a group!

Being able to figure out the hidden rules is a BIG part of being in any situation. We'll be talking a lot about hidden rules in other parts of the book. It's really important!

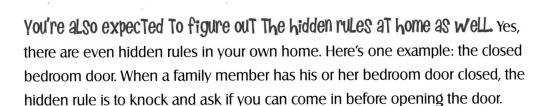

Figuring out the hidden rules is something you're expected to do whenever you're around other people.

Social Memory

Our brains have a special power called "memory." When we're babies, we don't have much memory because we haven't experienced very much. As we go through life, all the details of our experiences are stored in our brain so we can think about them again when needed. **Our memory gives us the ability to recall all that information.**

Our brains work the same way as we learn things about other people and have experiences with them.

When we use our brain to remember things about people and situations, we call this **using our social memory.** Our social memories can help us figure out what things might make other people happy and what will make others not so happy. Our social memories can also help us figure out what people might be interested in and even what they're not interested in. This helps us know what they might like to do or talk about. Remembering more about other people and how they feel about certain things will help us know what to do when we're with them. We want to do things the other person might like if we want that person to like us.

As we gather this information about other people and situations, we keep it in our brain. We can imagine that in our brain is a set of files that we can call our **"people files."** Every person we know has their own set of people files in their mind. As we meet and get to know others, our people files grow.

Using social memory isn't something only you have to do. Other people do this with you as well! Your parents and others in your family remember what you like and don't like, or what makes you feel good and bad. Your friends do this too. So don't think you're the only one having to use your social memory. **Everyone is expected to use their social memory to keep their relationships calm and enjoyable.**

Making a Smart Guess

Facts are things we know. For example, if you have brown hair, that's a fact. Where you live, where you go to school, and the names of the people in your family are all facts.

You learn many, many facts but not everything you learn is a fact. Especially when it's connected to people, some things you learn aren't "always true" in the same way facts are. These things change depending on the situation.

Sometimes you may find yourself in a situation when you have to make a guess. When you don't have much information, you might make a silly guess (also called a wacky guess). An example is if your aunt holds up a white box and asks you to guess what's inside. It could be almost anything: a taco, a map, a belt, a video game, or a deck of cards. You don't have much information to help you guess, so it's okay if your guess is silly or wrong. People don't expect you to always get it right when you have little information.

But sometimes you do have some information or you can find some clues to help you make a guess. You can make a **smart guess** when you use these two things together:

- What you know from past learning (facts or your social memory or both)

- Any clues you can find in the situation (by thinking with your eyes)

Sometimes you have to look for clues to make a smart guess in a situation.

Here are two examples of making a smart guess:

- Let's say you like to hang out with a person named Siddhartha. When you go outside for free time, you look for Siddhartha. You see Siddhartha is already playing a board game with three other kids. You make a smart guess that you won't be able to play with him this time because he's already playing with other kids. So you think about something else to do.

- It's lunchtime and you're in the cafeteria with three of your friends. You don't like the turkey sandwich your dad made for you that day. You decide to see if one of your friends will trade lunches. You use your social memory to re-member that Destin doesn't like turkey either. You make a smart guess that he won't want to trade. But Margaret loves turkey sandwiches, so you ask her instead.

In school students are expected to make smart guesses all the time in their classwork. Even when we're outside of class, like when we're playing sports or watching a game, we can make smart guesses about what's happening in the situation. We get better at making smart guesses each year we're alive. This is because over time we've gotten to do many different things. This means we've built up those memories in our brains. We remember what things look like, taste like, smell like, feel like, and sound like. Also, we remember the order in which things happen.

Adults use other words that mean pretty much the same thing as "making a smart guess." Some of these words are: "making a prediction" and "making your best estimate." A slang term you might hear is "giving it your best shot" when answering a question or figuring out a solution.

We can think with our eyes to make a smart guess about situations we see. What can you figure out here?

These Social Thinking Vocabulary words and ideas are a good start for now. Other chapters will explain more vocabulary words to help you think in more and more advanced ways about how we use our social thinking. Others will have good thoughts about you when you're a social thinker, and you'll feel good about yourself too!

Now, go explore how all this information applies to you in the Thinksheets book.

LeT's Recap ChapTer 3
Social Thinking Vocabulary

● To become a better social thinker, I can use special Social Thinking Vocabulary words to help me learn. I can also use these words and terms to talk about social ideas with others. They can help me be a better social detective to figure out what's happening at different places and with different people.

● I have thoughts about other people, and they have thoughts about me.

● My thoughts are connected to my feelings.

● I can think with my eyes to find social clues and cues in a situation. This means I look around AND then use my brain to think about what I'm observing.

● Situations have hidden rules in them. Different situations have different hidden rules.

● When I follow the hidden rules, I'm using behavior that helps people around me feel comfortable and calm.

● When I'm not following the hidden rules, my behavior is unexpected. Others may feel uncomfortable around me.

● Making smart guesses, especially about hidden rules, is one of the most important things I can learn to do as a social thinker.

● My teachers and parents know I'm working hard to become a social thinker. They'll feel proud as they see me using these tools to think in a social way.

Social Thinking Vocabulary

• Thoughts and feelings
• Thinking with your eyes
• Hidden Rules
• Social memory
• Smart guess

CHAPTER 4

We ALL Have FeeLings

The words "emotions" and "feelings" are often used together. Both are about how people feel inside their bodies.

How people feel inside affects how they react to things and people around them. If people feel happy, they tend to look happy (they smile). They also act happy. They might use a happy sounding voice, talk more, or move their arms and body more when they talk.

When people feel sad, they tend to look and act sad. Their face and mouth might sag a bit or their shoulders may droop. They might avoid looking at people and move slowly. They might choose not to be a part of activities with others and not talk very much. They might look like they want to cry.

We have To Learn To pay aTTenTion To how we feeL on The inside.

It helps to understand our own feelings before we can fully understand how other people feel. We each have feelings. Sometimes our feelings or emotions are there but we don't really know why we feel one way or another, like sad or happy. Other times it's very clear what makes us feel the way we do.

Many Times we don'T even reaLize we're having a feeLing! It's not like we have a computer system that gives us automatic updates on how we feel every 10 minutes. We have to learn to pay attention to how we feel on the inside. We have to start to connect what sadness feels like inside our bodies and how that feels different from feeling angry. Also, we need to learn how feeling sad or angry is different from feeling scared or happy or surprised. This takes practice! It's easy to see when we've cut our hand and we know it hurts. But it's not always easy to know what we're feeling on the inside when other things happen. An example is the hurt we feel when a friend doesn't invite us to the movies and instead goes with someone else.

People have many different emotions. Some of them are happy, sad, afraid, mad, excited, angry, and embarrassed.

Our feelings can also come in different sizes. Sometimes we might feel super happy. An example would be if our mom tells us we're going to Disney World. Sometimes we might feel just a little happy, like when our dog runs to greet us when we get home from school. In both situations, we feel happy but the feeling has a different size. Or we might feel a little proud for spelling a word correctly on a spelling quiz. But we'd probably have bigger proud feelings if we just won a spelling bee. The word "proud" describes what we're feeling in both situations but how that feels is different.

Sometimes we don't have much of a feeling at all. For instance, mom makes chicken for dinner. We don't hate chicken, and we don't love chicken, we just think it's "okay." We sometimes call that feeling "neutral."

How we feel can change the way we act!

Why is it so important to understand our emotions? Here's the big reason: how we feel can change the way we act. If we feel sad, we may not look very interested in what other people are doing. If we feel happy, we're more likely to connect with others and send them the message that we want to talk or play together. If we feel angry, we're more likely to show people our anger, even if they didn't cause it! That may make them feel uncomfortable and they may not want to be around us. If we feel surprised, we may appear as if we're not sure what's happening around us.

Figuring out our emotions is something we do all our lives. Take the time to practice noticing how you feel on the inside. Then try to pair that feeling with an emotion word, such as happy, sad, mad, scared, or worried. As you get better at doing this, you can start thinking about how you look to others when you feel different emotions. For instance, what happens to you when you get mad? Are your hands in a fist? Does your voice get louder? Do you stomp your feet? It's important to get better at noticing what *you* do and how *your* body and face look when you have a certain feeling. As you do, you'll also get better at noticing these same things in others. And that will help you understand how to figure out others' emotions as well!

SomeTimes iT's easy To figure ouT whaT oTher peopLe are feeLing. And SomeTimes iT's noT!

Sometimes it's easy to figure out what other people are feeling. You can listen to their words, look at their body posture, and watch their eyes. But other times it can be tricky because some people learn to "hide" what they're feeling from others. They may look happy on the outside but can be feeling sad on the inside. No matter what, it's always important to think about what others are feeling when you're with them.

What might these boys be thinking and feeling?

We look at other people's bodies to determine how they feel by looking at their face, arms, hands, and body position. Doing this plus using our brain to figure out the situation is called reading all the "nonverbal cues" to try and figure out what that person may be thinking and feeling.

To figure out what a person is feeling, you can first think with your eyes. You can look at the person to see what nonverbal messages his body is sending and to notice his facial expression. For example, is his body turned toward you or away? Is he looking at you or looking away from you? What's he doing with his hands? You can also try and notice if he's smiling, laughing, glaring, frowning, or pouting.

How is this situation different?

Next, you can think about what he's saying and how he's saying it. A person's tone of voice and how loud or soft it is often give clues about a person's emotions. For example, a loud volume can mean someone is excited, afraid, or angry. A tone of voice that keeps getting louder can mean someone is surprised, excited, or unsure. A soft volume may mean someone is shy or feeling unsure of what to say or do.

Body positions, facial expression, tone of voice, and voice volume are all different types of clues. These clues may be hard to notice if you're not looking or listening for them. Some signals can mean more than one thing. So it's also always important to be thinking about the situation to help you know for sure. (Remember, the " situation" means what's going on at that time and place and with the people who are involved.)

The emotions you have or that other people have are almost always connected to what we're thinking at the time, other people and their actions, and the situation. What another person is doing at the moment usually makes us and others feel a certain way. What a person has done in the past or plans to do in the future also makes us and others have different feelings.

Some behaviors in a situation may lead others to feel comfortable emotions such as happy, excited, relieved, or relaxed. Other behaviors in a situation may lead others to have not so pleasant feelings such as mad, annoyed, sad, frustrated, embarrassed, or impatient. Here's an example. Imagine you're building with Legos and you see your little sister running toward you. Because you remember that she likes to grab things you're using, you probably feel worried that she plans to grab some of your Legos this time too. If she does, she might ruin the mega-cool structure you just finished. That would probably make you feel angry. But, if your sister doesn't grab it and says, "Cool!" or even "Can I help?," you would probably feel relieved and maybe even proud.

When you're with other people, it's important to try to figure out how you're thinking and feeling. Then you can also try to figure out how other people are thinking and feeling.

This is all part of doing what is expected and being a good social thinker. We do this when we're in class, hanging out with friends, or standing in line. These thoughts and ideas help us know the best way to be around other people.

Think with your eyes to figure out what each person might be feeling.

In many ways, people try to be social detectives to figure out how they feel and how other people feel. To figure out how each of us feels, we may:

- Pay attention to our own body to see if we feel relaxed or stressed.

- Notice our thoughts. Are they good or bad about the situation we're in?

- Try to observe how we're reacting to others. Do people, or even just certain people, around us tend to make us feel grumpy or happy? When we feel good, we often like being with people more than when we feel bad.

- Ask a trusted adult to help us if our feelings seem confusing or unclear.

IT Takes pracTice To figure ouT how peopLe feeL in differenT siTuaTions. We don'T aLways geT iT righT!

To figure out how others feel, we may:

- Look at the situation and think about what it tells us. For instance, if we're at a funeral, many people may be feeling sad. If we're at the Olympics, many people may feel excited or hopeful.

- Look at other people to see how most people feel at that time. What clues can we see in their faces, bodies, and their voices that tell us what they may be feeling?

- Listen to the words people are using in their conversations. This is often a good clue about how other people are feeling.

● If someone doesn't look like she feels the same as everyone else, it might help to watch her more carefully. We want to try and understand why she may feel better or worse than the other people.

However, as much as we try to figure out other people and how they feel, we're not always right! Sometimes we get it wrong. It's easy to confuse different emotions such as sad and mad. Sometimes someone may be sad and pull away from a group of friends. When that happens, the other people in the group might think, "Oh, he must be mad at us for something because he isn't joining us." That's why it helps if we tell people how we feel, so they don't think something else is going on with us.

It's okay to feel sad, but you may not want to be with other people when you're sad. When you feel sad, you can tell people, "Sorry, I don't feel like talking today. I just don't feel that great." This helps people understand that you're not mad at them and just need some time to yourself.

We all remember how people make us feel. When someone does something that makes you feel good, you remember it, right? If that person does something that makes you feel bad, you remember that too, right? It's the same with other people. If you do something that makes others feel good, they may remember you as friendly. If you do something that makes others upset, they may remember you as rude or mean. Can you think of any times this happened to you?

It takes practice to figure out how people feel in different situations. Sometimes the clues are pretty clear and sometimes you'll have to work harder to figure things out.

Now, go explore how all this information applies to you in the Thinksheets book.

Let's Recap Chapter 4
We All Have Feelings

⚫ Everyone has feelings all the time, and there are many different types of feelings that people have.

⚫ It's really important to try and figure out my own feelings and tell people what I'm feeling if they ask. That will help other people understand what I might need.

⚫ As I get better at knowing my own feelings, I'll also get better at making smart guesses about how other people feel.

⚫ Our feelings come in different sizes. Sometimes people have big feelings, and sometimes people have small feelings.

⚫ People may feel a certain way because of what other people are doing in the moment. They also may have a certain feeling because they remember what another person has done in the past, or notice what someone might do next.

⚫ It can be hard to figure out what someone is feeling at first. My parents and teachers can help me do this when I'm not sure.

⚫ As I spend time with other kids and other people, it's usually important to act in a way that makes them feel good. When others feel good around me, they're more likely to remember me as friendly.

CHAPTER 5

Thinking With Your Eyes

So far We've Learned all sorts of Things about being a social Thinker.

We've learned that people use all of their senses, especially their eyes and ears, to help them notice what's going on around them. Then it's our brain's job to make sense of that information so we can figure out what to do or say in a situation.

KEEP IN MIND:

Thinking with
your eyes means
you're Looking
AND Thinking
about what
you're seeing.

We've also learned that all people (that includes you!) have feelings. Sometimes we share the same feelings in a situation and sometimes our feelings are different. Our behaviors are usually tied to our feelings, too. When people are happy, they mostly act happy. When people are mad, they mostly show their mad feelings by what they say or do. For instance, they might yell or say unkind things.

When we're around other people, it's important to think about the situation and the people in it and try to use flexible thinking. Social thinking = flexible thinking! That way we can do our best to be a good member of the group so that everyone feels comfortable being together.

In this chapter we're going to talk about another important social idea. It's called **Thinking with your eyes**. It means we use our eyes combined with our brain power to look at a situation and the people in the situation to figure out the meaning of what we're seeing. For example, you come into your class late and you see your teacher is teaching a lesson. You look closer and you notice all the kids have their Social Studies books on their desks and you then figure out that this is time for Social Studies. You may even make a smart guess to figure out you should go sit down and pull out your Social Studies book. No one had to tell you this—you just figured it out with your eyes!

You've probably heard people say "use good eye-contact", but when they tell you this you don't necessarily know you're supposed to do anything with your eyes except point them at a person's face. Thinking with your eyes actually means that when you look you're supposed to think about all you're seeing and try to make sense of what is going on around you!

Start to notice how well you most likely already do this! You watch people and you start to figure out how people feel, where people are going, and even what someone wants you to do next! As easy as this is to do sometimes, it can be hard to do at other times. For example, if you're staring at your cell phone or your portable gaming device it's hard to know what people are doing around you because you're not thinking with your eyes. For some students, their brains make it hard for them to use their eyes to look at people and notice what other people are doing, thinking or planning to do next.

Here's something really important to think about: Our eyes are like arrows. They point to what we're looking at. What we're looking at is connected to what we're thinking about. That's what thinking with your eyes is all about, in a very simple way. It's a strategy we can all use to help us figure out what's going on around us!

Thinking with your eyes can seem like a really big idea, and even people who do it pretty well don't realize that they do this at all! So let's break it down into different parts.

Why is it so important to think with your eyes?

People keep track of other people around them and think about why people are near them. One reason is for personal safety. We want to be able to get away from a person who might do us harm!

Another reason we keep track of people around us is to figure out what those people are doing and why. We think with our eyes and **look for clues** that give us more information. That helps us make a smart guess about why we're all together, what someone else is doing, and at times it helps us find clues to figure out what we should or shouldn't be doing. We call this **figuring out the group plan**.

Thinking with our eyes also helps us figure out expected and unexpected behavior.

This helps us do our part to keep the group moving along smoothly with everyone cooperating and feeling okay about being together. (Figuring out what's expected/unexpected is another key social idea and there's a whole chapter about it coming up next!)

When we think with our eyes, we can also zoom in on what people may be thinking about and how they're possibly feeling. If we know
what someone is looking at, this can help us make sense of what they're talking about! Imagine this: Your mom is looking at your dirty plate on the dinner table and she says, "Can you please put *that* in the sink!" You don't know what she means by "put that in the sink" unless you look at her eyes to notice what she's looking at (your plate) which helps you figure out what she's thinking about. Start to notice how many times people begin talking about things they're looking at, without ever explaining what they're talking about. You probably do this as well!

Another big reason we think with our eyes is to show people we're paying attention to them! People like it when we show we're interested in them, especially when we're working in a group, talking to a person or showing someone that we want to be friendly. Most people like to know that others want to be around them. You probably feel that same way too, right? We all do! It feels good when you know that someone else likes you and wants to be around you.

What do we look at when we think with our eyes?

Detectives collect clues to figure out what's going on with people around them. Every person is expected to be what we call a "social detective" to figure out what's going on with the people around them.

Here are some examples of how thinking with our eyes can help us figure some things out. Let's start with using our eyes and brain to help ourselves in a situation.

- If you see a clock, and the time is "11:50 a.m.", your brain can figure out it's almost time for lunch.

- If you see it's raining outside, you can figure out that you should bring your umbrella or raincoat when you go outside.

- If you think with your eyes and notice all your classmates are sitting quietly with their desks cleared, you can figure out that you should probably clear your desk and sit quietly too.

Social detectives always find clues about the situation they're in, the people around them and what those people might be thinking or planning to do next. All by thinking with their eyes! Here are some tips that detectives receive in their formal training.

Thinking with your eyes about the situation

There are usually a lot of details to notice in a situation. For example:

- What's the place? Is it a garden, a baseball field, a friend's house, or a boat? The place or setting gives us clues.

- What's in the place? This includes all the things you can see, such as a clock on a wall, colorful party decorations, piles of clothes on the floor, or bigger things, like a school bus, a wrecked car, or a firetruck.

- When we talk about the "situation" it means the same thing as when the teacher is talking about the "setting" in a book. If you're around people or just reading about them in a book, you'll always have to figure out what situation/setting they're in to make sense of how they're behaving!

What can you figure out about this situation?

Thinking with your eyes about the people in the situation

- Who is there? Are there lots of people or just a few? Are they strangers, friends, classmates, or your relatives? Are they kids or grown-ups?

- What are the people doing? Are they sitting, standing, running, talking, helping others, or maybe even being quiet and just listening?

- What are they planning? Can you figure out what they might do next?

- What feelings are the people showing? Do different people look happy or sad or frightened? Maybe there aren't a lot of feelings showing at all? Everyone has feelings but not everyone shows their feelings. Can you figure out how people feel even if they don't show it?

Try this right now: become a social detective. Think with your eyes, carefully scan, or look around the place you're in, and try to pick out the things that may give you more information about the situation. It's usually important to take your time doing this. If you look around too quickly, or don't look around closely enough, it's easy to miss some of the clues.

Another word for taking your time to look around is **observing**. Observing is an important skill to learn and become comfortable doing. As you observe your situation, notice the people around you. Is everyone doing what's expected in this situation? Is anyone doing what's unexpected? If so, why do you think they're doing that? How do you feel about that? How do you think your teacher or other students feel? Notice that you notice a lot of things you never talk about. All this thinking helps us be socially smart!

> Observing means taking your time to look around at the people and the situation you're in to find helpful clues about what's going on.

Let's review: the clues in each situation help us figure out all sorts of things like:

- What's going on? Why are people together in this place?

- What are other people doing?

- How are people feeling?

- What are the hidden rules in this situation? (Hidden rules are talked about too in the expected/unexpected chapter coming up.)

- What's the expected behavior? What's the unexpected behavior?

- What might happen next?

The older we get The more we're expected To Think wiTh our eyes To noTice whaT's going on.

Just like detectives look for clues to help them solve a mystery, when we're in a social situation we look for clues to help us figure out what to do and say. The older we get, the more we're expected to be really strong social detectives and think with our eyes to notice what's going on.

When people aren't great social detectives people may describe them as looking "spaced out." It's actually expected for us to notice what people are doing around us even when we have no plans to talk to them or become friends with them.

It takes a lot of practice to figure out what others are thinking and feeling. We may never know for sure, but we do use our eyes to make a lot of smart guesses. Remember: eyes are like arrows. What a person is looking at tells us what that person may be thinking about.

To figure out what another person is looking at we look at their body, their head, their face, and their eyes. We try to follow the direction their eyes are pointing and see if that's toward a person or an object. This can be hard to do sometimes, but it's important to try. The more you practice the better you'll get at doing this.

Figuring out what a person may be Thinking

Here are some more examples of thinking with your eyes to figure out what a person might be thinking:

- If your friend is looking at the teacher, he's probably thinking about the teacher.

- If your classmate is looking at his test, he's probably thinking about his test.

- If your teacher is looking at you, she's probably thinking about you!

- If your sister is looking at shoes at the mall, she's probably thinking about new shoes!

- If your friend is sitting at his desk but his head, face, and eyes are looking at the class outside the window, he's probably thinking about the class and maybe wondering where they're going.

- If your scout leader is looking at a fossil you all found on a field trip, he's probably thinking about the fossil and what he might know about it.

Figuring out Who Someone is Talking To

We can think with our eyes to also figure out who someone is talking to. We do this by looking at the direction that a person's shoulders or face are turned and combine that with where their eyes are pointing. This is usually a clue about who the person is talking to.

- If your friend's face and shoulders are turned toward the teacher, she's probably talking to the teacher.

- If your teacher is standing near one student or a small group of students working on a project and her head and shoulders are turned toward the individual or the group while the teacher is talking, she's probably talking to that person or group, not the whole class.

- However, if your teacher is at the front of the room and she's facing everyone while she's talking, even if students are working in small groups, the teacher is probably saying something to the entire class.

- If you and two friends are walking side by side toward the soccer field and one friend is talking about his vacation to Florida, it's expected that he's looking in the direction he's walking but he's still talking to you while he's thinking about his vacation in Florida.

We can think with our eyes to look for **clues that another person's body parts are sending.** Often people communicate using gestures, facial expressions, and body movements. When we notice these things, we can figure out what they're trying to say. (We'll talk more about this in Chapter 7: Keeping My Body, Eyes, Ears, and Brain in the Group.)

- When someone nods, it may mean that he agrees or is interested in what another person is saying.

- When someone points, it may mean that he wants us to look somewhere or go somewhere.

- When someone waves, it could mean "hello" or "come here" or even "goodbye."

- When someone puts his hand out with his palm facing you, it may mean "stop" what you're doing (talking, moving toward him, etc.).

- When someone is sitting quietly with his eyes closed and his hands folded together in his lap, his body sends the message that he probably doesn't want to talk or be disturbed.

Figuring out What To say To another person

We can think with our eyes to help us figure out what to say to another person **or even if we should say anything at all!**

- If you notice someone is wearing something interesting, you can ask a question to find out more about it. For example, if a person's shirt says "NYC" you could ask, "Have you ever been to New York City?"

- If you notice someone is reading a book that you've read, you can tell that person, "I've read that book too! I liked it."

- If you notice two kids are playing a video game and are really excited about it, thinking with your eyes tells you it might not be a good time to ask them about your math homework.

Figuring ouT The group pLan

We can think with our eyes to figure out the group plan or guess what another person's plan might be.

When we use our eyes to look at another person's body position and actions we can find clues about what he or she might do next.

- If your teacher is holding a marker, and standing in front of the white-board, chances are she's about to write something on the board.

- If your mother has just poured herself a bowl of cereal, and is holding a spoon, she's probably about to eat that cereal.

- If your friend just unzipped her backpack, and is reaching her hand inside that backpack, she's probably about to take something out.

- If you're at a friend's birthday party and she's sitting in front of her cake, she's probably getting ready to blow out the candles.

- If you see your dad looking in the refrigerator, and you just asked him for the milk, chances are he's probably getting the milk.

- If you see all the kids in the auditorium get up and start walking toward the exit, you can figure out the group plan is to go back to class because the assembly is over.

There are many reasons to think with our eyes. It's something people do all the time when they're working in a group, hanging out with others, or doing something together. And here's something else to consider:

you Think with your eyes even when you don'T plan To Talk To or interacT with oTher people you're around!

You do this because you still need to figure out the expected behaviors when you're around others. Thinking with your eyes is a way to gather clues about the situation and the people in the situation to help you figure all this out. Using all this information, you're becoming an even better social detective, meaning you're practicing making smart guesses about what to do or say yourself! That's cool!

Now, go explore how all this information applies to you in the Thinksheets book.

LeT's Recap ChapTer 5
Thinking with Your Eyes

- When I'm with other people, it's always important to think with my eyes. This means I look around at where I am, notice the person or people I'm near or with, and notice what's going on.

- There are many reasons to think with my eyes. Doing this can help me:

  - Be safe

  - Figure out what people are doing and why

  - Figure out what I'm supposed to be doing in a situation

  - Let others know I'm interested in them

  - Let others know I'm paying attention

- When I take my time to think with my eyes about a situation, I'm observing and learning to use my social detective skills.

  - There are all sorts of things I can do once I learn to think with my eyes. I can:

    - start a conversation with someone

    - make a guess about another person's plan

    - figure out how someone is feeling

    - figure out what I should be doing or not doing!

  - Thinking with my eyes is not something I do just once, and then I'm done. It's a strategy I'll use all throughout my day and anywhere I am: at school, at home, during recess or breaks, at the mall or anywhere else I find myself.

CHAPTER 6

Thinking About The Hidden RuLes and ExpecTed BehaVior

Wherever we go and in every situation we find ourselves, we use our social detective skills to notice and think about our own behaviors and those of others.

Behaviors include our actions, our facial expressions, our words and tone of voice. Our behaviors can be expected or unexpected.

Expected behavior is behavior that most people do in a certain place or certain situation.

Unexpected behavior is the opposite. It's behavior that most people wouldn't do in a situation and isn't expected.

KEEP IN MIND:

Expected behavior in one situation may be different than expected behavior in another situation.

Figuring out the hidden rules helps you know what is expected in any situation!

Very often, no one tells us exactly what the hidden rules (expected behaviors) are. We mostly have to figure this out for ourselves. Sometimes though, when we're younger, adults teach us rules to follow that are another way of helping us learn what's expected and unexpected. One example you've probably heard is that you need to stay quiet when someone else is talking.

Expected and unexpected behaviors are sort of the rules about a situation or place. We say "sort of" because what is expected and unexpected in one situation can be different than what's expected or unexpected in another situation. It's important to keep in mind that expected/unexpected behavior depends on the situation we're in and the people in it.

In most situations, expected behavior makes other people feel happy, safe, and relaxed. People have good thoughts about others when they have expected behavior and are following the hidden rules. People like being with people who use expected behavior.

Unexpected behavior often makes others feel confused, annoyed, worried, or sad. People have uncomfortable thoughts about others when they have unexpected behavior. People may not want to be with others who use unexpected behavior.

Watching TV at home—unexpected behavior

Here are some examples of expected and unexpected behavior. Remember that the expected behavior is the same as a hidden rule for that situation.

- In a library, it's expected behavior (a hidden rule) to use a quiet voice and move our body carefully around people and computers. Running and shouting in a library, or even talking loudly, is unexpected behavior.

- It can be expected behavior on a schoolyard to use a loud voice, run around, and throw a ball. But pushing others, not sharing the ball, or knocking down or destroying what other kids are working on is considered unexpected behavior.

Expected behavior (hidden rules) in a group with other people usually means using friendly behavior:

- Using kind words and a friendly voice

- Keeping your body and actions under control while staying with others in the group

- Asking before touching things that belong to someone else

- Listening while others are talking

- Thinking with your eyes

Expected behavior while in a group usually means using friendly behavior.

Some unexpected behaviors in a group with other students are:

- Not sharing

- Only playing what you want to play

- Touching others in unfriendly ways such as pushing, hitting, kicking, or grabbing

- Using unkind words or calling other kids names

- Interrupting others when they're talking

- Invading someone's personal space, for example, leaning on someone or bumping into a person again and again

Figuring out the hidden rules of what's expected and unexpected in a certain place or at a certain time isn't always easy, but you can do it. The first step is to think with your eyes about the situation. If you remember from an earlier chapter, this is called observing or being a social detective. A good social detective can figure out what's expected and unexpected behavior by looking at the situation and finding the social clues. A good social detective will also try and do the expected behavior!

Expected behavior in a group.

Unexpected behavior in a group.

Figuring out The hidden ruLes.

But what if you're not sure about what the expected behavior is in a situation? It's a good idea to look around and notice what other people are doing. You're thinking with your eyes and ears again! You'll use this a LOT! This means when you see and hear things, you use your brain to think about what most people are doing. You may ask yourself questions like these:

- Are most people sitting or standing?

- Are most people talking, not talking, shouting, etc?

- Are people moving around or doing different things?

You can also always ask your parents or teachers about the hidden rules. Your parents and teachers know you're working hard to learn and use expected behavior. Your questions and efforts show them you're learning to use your social thinking!

Now, go explore how all this information applies to you in the Thinksheets book.

LeT's Recap Chapter 6
Thinking About the Hidden Rules and Expected Behavior

- It's important to figure out the hidden rules of any situation. The hidden rules help me to know what behavior is expected of me.

- When I follow the hidden rules, I'm doing what most people expect me to do in that place or situation. When I use expected behavior, most people feel happy and relaxed.

- When I use unexpected behavior in a situation, I'm not following the rules for that situation. Some of these are hidden rules that people are expected to understand. When I use unexpected behavior, people will probably have some not-so-good feelings like annoyed, nervous, confused, or even worried.

- I'll try to remember that it's important to figure out what the expected behavior is and then use it. I can do this by thinking with my eyes or by asking for help.

CHAPTER 7

Keeping My Body, Eyes, Ears, and Brain in The Group

Have you ever been in a group and one person doesn't seem to be paying attention? Maybe the person is thinking of other things...

Maybe the person's head and body is turned away from others and the person is looking at something else while you're all talking. Did you feel distracted or annoyed by what the person was doing? Most of us would have that reaction.

When we're sharing space with other people in a group it's expected that we pay attention to what's going on around us. We also have to think about what people expect from us. In this chapter we'll learn more about ways we can use our bodies, eyes, ears and brain as we share space with others to show them we're in the group and following the group plan.

Why does it matter if other people think I'm part of the group? I know I am!

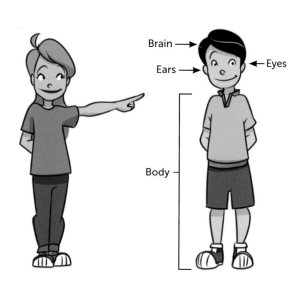

Brain
Ears
Eyes
Body

When groups work well together, everyone is following the same group plan. Here's the thing: most people can tell when someone is part of the group and they can tell when someone is not part of the group. How? They look at a person's body, eyes, and actions and then use their brain to figure it out. Our bodies send silent messages to others in different ways. These are clues we can learn to notice and think about.

We all think with our eyes to see if people are interested in us. People who are leading the group may be using their eyes to see if you're interested in them! Most of us don't

like it if we're trying to talk to someone or a group of people and we notice that a person is looking anywhere but toward us! Next time you're with another person, notice how you feel if someone isn't paying attention to you. Often this makes people feel frustrated or mad. It seems like the person who is "spaced out" just doesn't seem to care about you.

When am I in a group?

Before going any further, let's define a "group." **A group is more than one person sharing the same space or interacting in a situation.** A group can be as small as two people or a group can be lots of people together! Most of the time a group has a group plan. That means everyone is together for a common reason. For instance, all the kids in your class form a group and the plan is to learn new things. A baseball team is a group with the purpose of playing the game. Some friends may be hanging out together after school with the group plan to just show each other they're included with each other. When we're with others, even when we're not talking much to each other, we're still a group.

Here's something interesting to think about: unless you're completely by yourself physically away from everyone else, the rest of the time you're in some sort of a group. Being in a classroom with the other students means you're to follow the plan of that group; if you're in line in the cafeteria, you have to follow the group plan of the kids in the line, etc. That means each person is expected to think about how to interact with others in the group. Constantly!

Groups work best when everyone is following the group plan.

Part 1:

The messages our bodies send to others

We use our bodies in many different ways to establish physical presence and let people know our plan is to be part of the group. This means we communicate with more than just our words!

KEEP IN MIND:

We communicate with more than just our words! Our bodies send messages too.

1. **We use our body to show *directional signals*.** For instance, when we first enter a group we want our toes, hips, shoulders, and head facing toward the other persons and our eyes looking toward the face of one or more people in the group. We also make sure our body is spaced about one arm's length between the persons standing next to us, on each side. Together all of these things are called being **physically present**. When we're physically present, this communicates without words that we're interested in the other person or persons.

2. Our eyes combined with our hands and arms can also serve as **direction signals to what we're thinking about.** For instance, we might use our arm, hand, and finger to point to our tablet as we say, "Hey look at this cool app I found!" while also looking with our eyes between the app itself and the people who we want to look at the app. Our eyes help to serve as a leash. We tend to keep people thinking about us and what we find interesting if we use our eyes along with our body to help control what other people are paying attention to!

3. **When we want to leave a group, we also communicate with our eyes and body** by turning our eyes, head, shoulders, arms, hips, and feet away from the group as we move away.

4. **We communicate to others through our *body language*.** You probably already recognize when people use gestures to communicate nonverbally. For instance, we can use our shoulders to shrug as a way to say, "I don't know." We use our head to nod agreement or shake it back and forth to say "no." Each person uses body language a little differently. Even so, there are certain ways we use our bodies that pretty much everyone understands and that are part of figuring out the hidden rules for a situation. (We talk more about the hidden rules of body in the group/out of the group later in the chapter.)

5. **We can also send a message just by how close or far we stand from others.** When we're standing in a group, how far we stand makes a difference. If we want to be included in a group but we stand six feet away from people and have our body turned away from them, the people in the group may think we actually don't like them or don't want to be with them! Typically we apply the one arm's length rule, which means we stand approximately one arm's length away from others while also facing our head, eyes, shoulders, hips, and feet in their direction.

6. **Be flexible on figuring out how near or far to stand or sit when with other people!** The actual "rules" on physical distance may vary based on culture, what you know about people (you stand closer to your sister, brother or parent), or a specific situation. While most often the one arm's length rule applies, if we're in a really small space, more squished together, then the rule may shift and we may stand only a half arm's length. If we're sitting together on the floor, our hips may actually come close to touching each other if it is a small space. Being in a big space with others is when people usually stand about one arm's length away from each other.

7. One thing is for sure: **when we're standing in a group, each person tries to stand about the same distance from each other.** So if one person is squished between two people, then everyone should be squished together, of if one person is one arm's length away then everyone should be one arm's length away. You can think with your eyes to notice this and figure out what to do when you're around other people.

Here are some examples of using your body, eyes, ears, and brain to let people know you're interested in them and want to be part of the group.

● When you're sitting in a classroom you turn your face, eyes, and body toward the teacher while she's teaching a lesson. That tells her you're listening with your ears and thinking with your eyes about her and what she's teaching.

● Your teacher is also using body language when communicating with you. If you're not looking at the teacher while she speaks, you'll miss this. Let's imagine your teacher says, "Fishing is an important industry in this part of Canada" as she points to a map. You might hear her words but if you don't look to see where she's pointing, you probably won't learn which region she's talking about.

When you're in a group with other people, like a work group at school, or when you're just hanging out with friends, you keep your body, face, and eyes turned in the direction of the people you're with.

As you go about your day today, think with your eyes to start to notice all the signals your social detective can read to figure out if someone is paying attention to you or to your teacher!

Adding our brain into The group

When we notice social clues by thinking with our eyes or listening with our ears, these signals don't really help us if we can't make sense of them! If someone is waving while jumping up and down and your brain doesn't know what that signal means, then you can't figure out what they're communicating and if their signal is even for you! This is where our brain comes in! **We use our brain to connect all the signals we're getting from our eyes and ears** as we pay attention to what people say, what people do, and how they look (we even use our nose, which is why you need to keep clean!). When we do this our brain is taking what it knows and making smart guesses. This helps us interpret what we think people are communicating.

We can even figure out what people are planning to do next if we use our brain power well. Weirdly, people don't usually tell us exactly what they're thinking, feeling or planning! Notice how many times your teacher walks toward something to send a signal to the class that she wants you to pay attention to something different in the

Our brain heLps us interpret whaT we Think peopLe are communicaTing. We're making a smarT guess!

room. You can possibly "read her plan" if you're paying attention to what she's looking at and the direction her body is moving, even if she doesn't tell you what she's about to do next!

Your parents and other kids around you send these types of signals. You also send these signals to others! That's why our brain is so important when we're with other people; it helps us figure out what others are doing and what we should be doing too!

When our body, eyes, ears, and brain are in the group, we're more likely to be listening and paying attention to others around us. And it's more likely that other people will notice we're listening too.

But—when one or more parts of our body or our brain are out of the group, people may think we're not listening or paying attention to them. Here are a couple of examples.

KEEP IN MIND:

When our body, eyes, ears, and brain are in The group, we're more LikeLy To be LisTening and paying aTTenTion To oThers.

1. **Times when we "space out."** You've probably noticed that our brain has to constantly do so much work and at times it gets tired. When we're not doing a good job thinking with our eyes and listening with our ears, this is called "being spaced out." It's called this because when people look at you they can see that you appear to be "off in space" and you're clearly not paying attention to what's going on around you. Everyone spaces out at times, even your teachers! Even so, most people don't like it when other people appear spaced out when we're trying to talk to them. And others don't like it when we're the ones who appear spaced out either! It's impossible to think with your eyes, keep your body in the group, listen with your ears, and read the group plan when your brain is off in space!

2. **Times when we're bored or not interested.** It's hard to keep our body, eyes, ears, and brain in the group when we're tired or we're just not interested in the people or the situation around us! This is when we tend to think (and hopefully not say out loud!), "This is boring." The thing is, we don't like people to show us that we're boring them! We really like people to be interested in what we're doing or saying. So when it comes to the "boring moment" it's still expected that you work to keep your body, eyes, ears, and brain in the group. You may take a little break to space out for a moment, but then work to get yourself re-focused on what's going on around you. This helps people feel like you're working hard to be a good member of the group and that you want to do your part to make others feel comfortable as you share space with them.

As you work to think with your eyes, listen with your ears, and keep your brain and body in the group, you're helping yourself notice what's going on around you. This helps you do what's expected. Notice that you like it when other people are doing this as well. Groups work best when everyone is trying to read and follow the group plan together.

In the rest of this chapter you'll find a LOT of information about expected/unexpected behaviors for keeping your body, eyes, ears, and brain in the group. Take your time reading these sections and see if you can start making sense of the different ways we send messages to others and use signals from others to figure out the social situation we're in.

Even when you're bored it's expected that you try to keep your body, eyes, ears, and brain in the group.

PART 2:
HIDDEN RULES (EXPECTED BEHAVIORS)
Body, Eyes, Ears, and Brain in the Group

First, let's remember that hidden rules are clues to the behaviors that are expected in the situation. This is an important idea to keep in mind as you read the different situations and examples that follow.

Look for the "Expected" icon below ("icon" means a graphic or picture). It's a clue that you're reading about hidden rules and expected behavior for that situation!

We'll start with some of the hidden rules (expected behavior) about keeping our body, eyes, ears, and brain in the group. After that we'll talk a little about what it looks like when we don't follow the hidden rules and behaviors that are unexpected.

HIDDEN RULES of wanting to be with one other person (body, eyes, ears, and brain in the group)

SITUATION: let's imagine you want to talk to one other person, like someone in your class or on the playground.

1. Think with your eyes to look for the person you want to be with.

2. Read the hidden rules to figure out if this is the right time and place to talk to the person.

a. Is the person alone or is the person busy talking to another person? If so, this may (or may not) be a good time to join them.

b. If you think it is a good time, walk slowly toward that person.

c. As you approach, say "hi" or use some other greeting.

3. Once you come up to the person, have your toes, hips, shoulders, and head facing him or her.

4. Stand about one arm's length away from the person.

5. Use your eyes to think about the person. This means you look at the person's face to figure out if he or she is thinking about you.

a. For instance, is the other person's body facing you and is the other person looking at you? That tells you the person is interested in YOU! You also do this to show the person you want to be with him or her.

6. Once you have figured out that the person is thinking about you, and you're using your body, face and eyes to show the other person you want to be with him or her, you can listen to what the person may say to you or others in the group or you can say something and start the discussion or conversation.

7. It would be unexpected if you just started talking while the other person was looking off somewhere else or the person's body was turned away. Those clues tell you the person is thinking about something or someone else or the person is not choosing to be with you.

HIDDEN RULES of joining a larger group that is standing (body, eyes, ears, and brain in the group with two or more other people)

SITUATION: You're joining a group of people who are already working or hanging out as a group.

1. Observe the group you want to join.

2. Notice if there is a "hole" in the group; a "hole" is a larger space between two people that makes it easier for you to enter with your body. If there is not a hole, is there a person you know in the group who you could say "hi" to as you enter, so they make space for you in the group?

3. As you enter into the group, have your toes, hips, shoulders, and head face the middle of where the other people are standing. Usually, everyone stands so they're turned toward the center of the group. As a new person enters the group, it is expected that people make room by shifting their bodies to open a space for you to enter the group.

4. Stand about one arm's length away from the other people, unless the group doesn't have a lot of space and then people will stand closer than the normal one arm rule. You can try to stand about the same distance as you see others standing next to each other.

5. Notice who is talking in the group. Think with your eyes to look toward the speaker. When different people speak in the group, shift your eyes to keep thinking about the speaker's face, mouth, and eyes. You can also look around a bit in the group, but you keep most of your attention on the speaker.

6. If someone asks a question, think with your eyes to see who that person is talking to. It might be you! If it is, answer the question and use your eyes to look toward the person who asked you the question. You can look at others a bit as well.

HIDDEN RULES of sitting in a group like a classroom (body, eyes, ears, and brain in the group)

SITUATION: your teacher wants you to pay attention to her while you sit in the classroom and she speaks to the entire class.

1. Sit with your body facing the teacher or the person talking (head, shoulders, trunk, arms, and legs).

2. Keep your hands on your desk, your feet on the floor, and your body mostly sitting up. It's okay to slump a bit.

3. Keep your face turned toward the person speaking. This helps you think and listen with your eyes and ears!

4. Keep your arms and legs "quiet." It's expected that you try to keep your body still enough so the teacher and the kids around you can concentrate. When you move your body parts around too much this is called "being distracting." People will probably think you're not listening or that you're bored with what they're saying. There's also a good chance you're distracting yourself from understanding what the speaker is saying.

5. The one exception to this is if you use a fidget to keep your brain focused. Some people's brains get distracted easily and if they have one object to fidget with under their desk, such as a Koosh ball, it can help keep their brain focused. This works as long as they think with their eyes on the speaker and not on the Koosh ball or whatever fidget is chosen!

HIDDEN RULES of keeping your brain in the group

Keeping your brain in the group basically means you're concentrating on what is going on around you. Teachers and/or others can see you're keeping your brain in the group when you:

1. Nod your head from time to time

2. Take notes about what the teacher is saying

3. Raise your hand to add a comment

4. Ask a question about what's being talked about

5. Look toward the student the teacher calls on to talk

Here's one last thing to think about when you're around others in a group. We're not always sitting or standing in one place. Sometimes people move around together and when they do, it's still expected that people keep their bodies and brains in the group.

HIDDEN RULES of keeping your body, eyes, ears, and brain in a group that's moving around.

SITUATION: You're with others and the group is moving around.

⚫ You're playing basketball with some friends. This is constant movement!
To be part of the team, it's expected that you:

· think with your eyes

· watch for signals from your team members

· keep your body moving in the same direction as the team

· listen to the things your team members are saying

· work together to score points

- You walk in a line, one classmate behind the other, to the library.

  · You walk without touching others

  · You stay about one arm's length away from others

  · Your eyes focus on looking where you're going

- The teacher says it's time to pick groups to work in.

  · You quickly stand up and look at a person you want to work with

  · If that person is looking in your direction and then appears to acknowledge you, give him or her a quick little smile in return

  · You then walk right over to that group. This communicates you want to work with the person.

  · If you want to work with a person but that person is not looking at you and seems to be paying attention to another person, this likely means the person plans to work with someone else. In that case, look around the room and see who is looking for a work partner.

- You and three other classmates are heading outside for recess or break.

  · You walk about the same speed as the other kids

  · You try to avoid touching or standing too close

  · You think about what is being talked about. You ask a question or make a comment about the topic everyone is talking about.

  · You mostly look ahead as you all walk side by side to your new location.

PART 3:

UNEXPECTED BEHAVIORS:

Body, eyes, ears, and brain in the group

The hidden rules tell us about expected behaviors. But there are times when we, or other people, don't know the hidden rules or don't follow the hidden rules. Those are the times we do things that are unexpected, that make others feel uncomfortable being around us. Look for the "Unexpected" icon below. It is a clue that a behavior is unexpected when you're around others.

Here's some information about what it looks like if you break the hidden rules about keeping your body, eyes, ears, and brain in the group.

You're standing more than one arm's length away.

When you do this your body position sends the message that you don't want to join the group or that people in the group make you feel uncomfortable. This may not be what you mean, and that's why it's important to think about the distance your body is to others and how they may interpret that.

⬤ You want to play four-square. You stand many feet away from the other kids playing four square and you're also far away from the kids standing in line to play. You're so far out of the group that no one thinks you want to play, even though you're watching them and you really do wish they would include you!

Your toes, hips, shoulders, or head are turned away from the people in the group, even a little bit.

People may think this means you aren't interested in what the group is saying or doing or you want to get away from them. Remember: your body sends silent messages that others interpret. They are thinking about you at the same time you're thinking about them!

⬤ Your teacher is talking to you after class. Your body is turned toward her, and you're listening to what she's saying, but you keep turning your head to look toward the door because your friend is waiting for you so you can go get lunch. Your teacher will think you're not paying attention to her and what she's saying to you.

You wander away from the group, even if you can still hear what others are saying.

When your body is no longer part of the group, your behavior sends nonverbal messages that can make people have uncomfortable thoughts about you. If you want others to think you're interested in them, wandering away from the group is unexpected behavior!

⬤ You and a few other classmates are standing around outside after school. While the other kids talk about what they plan to do on the weekend, you move a few feet away and sit down on the grass. You're tired! Even though you can still see them and hear what they're saying, your body is out of the group and your peers will think you're not interested in them and don't want to be included in their plans.

You're sitting too far away from others.

- You sit down at a table in the cafeteria where other kids are seated. But there are one or two empty seats between you and the other kids. Your body isn't with that group. People probably think you don't really want to be part of their group or that you're not comfortable joining their group. (Tip: If you're sitting a couple of seats away from others and they start to talk to you, you can move closer into an empty seat. This will show them you want to join their group by bringing your body closer to theirs.)

- You and your class go to the library and the librarian asks you all to get a chair and put it into a circle. You sit in a chair over at a table and you look at a book of interest to you. The librarian sees that you did not include yourself in the group and you're not listening with your eyes and ears, like everyone else. This is unexpected behavior. She thinks you're communicating you don't want to be there and you don't want to work with her or the others in your class.

You're standing too close to people.

When you stand too close to people you're with, it can make them uncomfortable. If you stand closer than one arm's length away from others and/or you start to touch others, this makes people feel very nervous! People usually respond to these uncomfortable feelings by moving a little bit away. Or they may say, "Could you move back, you're standing too close!" or "Please stop touching me!" If people say these things to you, take them seriously. A person may become really upset if he's touched when he doesn't want to be touched.

You're staring at others.

When around others, it is expected you pay attention to the speaker. However, if your eyes are constantly looking at the face of someone else or at some part of this person's body, this will make that person feel uncomfortable. This is called staring. It's an unexpected behavior to stare and a hidden rule is "don't stare." Even if we're friends with a person, it makes people feel uncomfortable if we stare. (The expected behavior is that you shift your eyes back and forth from the speaker to something or someone else and back again to the speaker. That's done pretty slowly because you don't want your eyes to look like ping-pong balls jumping around too quickly. That would be unexpected!)

Your brain is out of the group.

Your eyes are looking all over the place and aren't focused on the faces or hand gestures of the other people in the group. For example: You're in the classroom and your teacher is talking. You keep looking at the clock. Your brain is out of the group because you're thinking about the clock or the time, not your teacher's words. That's unexpected.

Here's another example. You and two other friends are at the mall. As you walk from store to store you're texting another friend on your phone while you walk along. Even though your body is in the group, your brain is out of the group because it's focused on your texts, not what your friends are saying.

You make comments or ask questions about things that are completely unrelated to what the group is talking about or doing.

● Let's imagine your teacher is talking to the class about the big lions in Africa. You raise your hand and say, "My dad just got a new car." In Social Thinking Vocabulary, this is called making a **whopping topic change**. (Whopping means big/huge/gigantic.) It's called that because your comment isn't related at all to what the group is learning about or talking about. This type of behavior is unexpected. It makes people feel uncomfortable and may make them have uncomfortable thoughts about you.

You're distracted. Something else keeps grabbing your attention.

● You're playing a video game with two other friends. You keep looking at what's happening on the television in another part of the room. You're distracted. Your brain is out of the group because you're not focusing on the other kids and the game. This will probably make the other kids in your group feel annoyed because you're not paying attention to the group plan.

● You invite a friend over to your house to study together. While you're together you keep checking Facebook to see what your other friends are up to. This behavior is unexpected, since the reason you're together is to study. Your friend will probably feel annoyed with you.

You're not moving along with the group.

- You and another classmate are on an errand for your teacher. You're going to the school office to pick up some new books for the class. As you walk to the office you look straight ahead, you walk a little faster than the other kid and you don't say anything to your classmate or look at him, even when he tries to talk to you. Your behavior is thought of as "unfriendly" as it sends a message to your classmate that you don't like being around him and you don't want to talk to him.

- You're in the classroom. Your teacher asks everyone to line up at the door. You stay at your desk. Your body is out of the group and your brain doesn't look like it's in the group either! This will make your teacher and the other kids wonder why you're not following the group plan. They will feel uncomfortable.

- You and some other kids are at soccer practice. The coach tells all the kids to break into two groups and sit down. You join a group then decide to lie down on the grass instead and think about your new video game. The other kids and your coach probably feel uncomfortable about your behavior. They may think you don't want to play soccer and be at the practice.

Remember, people don't know you want to be part of their group unless you show them. Keeping your body, eyes, ears, and brain working together are powerful tools to show others you're thinking about them. When you do this, people are more likely to feel relaxed and have neutral to good thoughts about you. They may even want to spend time with you again in the future.

Expected

Unexpected

Now,
go explore
how all this
information
applies to you in
the Thinksheets book.

Let's Recap Chapter 7
Keeping My Body, Eyes, Ears, and Brain in the Group

- Whenever I'm around one or more people, I'm in a group. Groups work best when everyone is trying to read and follow the group plan together.

- There are hidden rules about being in a group. The hidden rules help me figure out expected behavior for being in the group.

- It's expected that I use my body, eyes, ears, and brain together whenever I'm around others. There are also things I can do that show others I'm interested in being around them.

- When I am standing with others my body is in the group when it is about one arm's length away from others. I've also turned my feet, legs, trunk, shoulders, arms, and head toward the group. My eyes are thinking about others and then often looking in the direction of the person speaking.

- When I am sitting in a classroom, my body is in the group when my shoulders and face are turned toward the teacher (or the person talking), I'm thinking with my eyes while looking at the teacher, and my hands, arms, legs, and feet are quiet and calm.

- I keep my brain in the group by making sure my attention and thoughts are focused on the situation and the people in the situation. This includes listening to what others are saying, looking at what they're doing, and thinking about what they're feeling and thinking. I can make comments, ask questions about the topic or the situation, or use body language like nodding my head, to show others my brain is in the group.

- When my body, eyes, ears, and brain are in the group, I'm showing others that I care about the group or the community I am in. This makes everyone feel comfortable being together.

CHAPTER 8

Thinking of OThers Versus JUST Me

When you're around OTher PeopLe, talking, playing, or just sharing space, what you do helps people stay comfortable.

KEEP IN MIND:

IT'S OK To be a JUST Me person when you're noT sharing space with oTher peopLe.

That means you have to use your social thinking whenever you're around other people, even if you don't know them!

You may be wondering, "Do I have to do this ALL the time? Aren't there some times when it's okay to do just what I want to do and NOT think about others?" The good news is yes, there is! Keep reading!

When you're by yourself and not sharing space with other people, that's a time when you can be a JUST ME. Being a Just Me person means you can do what you want to do. You may not need to ask or notice what someone else is thinking or wants to do because you're alone. For example, when you're in your room by yourself reading, drawing, or listening to music, most of the time it's okay to be a Just Me.

Being a Just Me person is okay sometimes.

You can read the pages you want, choose the music you like, and use the app you want. This is okay because most things you do won't disrupt others. (If you're playing drums or loud music, that's something that might affect others!)

When you're around other people, it's important to be a Thinking of Others person. A Thinking of Others person means you think about your behavior and how it makes others think and feel. When you're a Thinking of Others person, you try to think about the other people who are sharing space with you. You also try to think about the people who will be in that same space later.

But when you're around other people, be a Thinking of Others person!

When you're around other people, it's important to be a Thinking of Others person.

Here's something to think about. Sometimes when you share space with others, you may not even be talking or hanging out with those people in any direct way. You may just be near them. For instance, you may be in the kitchen at home and the rest of the family is in the living room. Even though you're not in the same room, you're still sharing space in your house and need to use your social thinking. When your classmates are taking a test, you're sharing space even though no talking is allowed.

Here's something even more important to think about. **Even when people are just around each other, they have thoughts and feelings about people in that space!** During a test, all of your classmates are still aware of the other students around them. If someone does something unexpected, like hums during the test, everyone will have a thought about it and a feeling. They may feel annoyed or frustrated because they can't concentrate.

It's important to be a Thinking of Others person because when you are, other people feel calm and safe in your presence. Some people may even have good thoughts about you, such as a teacher or a parent. This is because they know how hard people have to work to cooperate with each other. Cooperation means we may need to change our own thoughts and behaviors so we do what's expected in the situation. Or, we do things that make it easier for people to work together in a group.

Being a JUST Me person around others Leads To unexpected behavior

as people may perceive you're selfish and this can make others feel upset, worried, disappointed, and even annoyed. People usually have uncomfortable thoughts when someone acts like a Just Me when they're around others.

Here are some examples of being a Thinking of Others or a Just Me person:

- You're a Thinking of Others person when you share your games, art materials, and other things because you know the other kids would probably like it if you do. It's no fun when someone keeps all their things to themselves!

  When you don't share, and expected behavior for the situation is to share, you're being a Just Me person.

Is the boy with the football being a Just Me or a Thinking of Others person? How can you tell?

You're being a JUST Me when you don't ask others about their thoughts, opinions, or what they want to do.

- You're a Thinking of Others person when you ask what games or things other people might like to play or do. This is because everyone likes to be asked their opinions. When you don't care or don't ask about what others want to do, you're being a Just Me person.

- When your mom is on the phone, you're a Thinking of Others person when you talk in a quiet voice when you're talking to people around your mom. You do this because you know it will help her hear the person she's talking to. This is called "being polite" and "using good manners." It will help her feel comfortable.

- When you don't notice what others around you are doing and act in a way that isn't polite, you're being a Just Me person. Another way to think about this is when you do things that make it hard for people to do what they're doing. For example, if you talk loudly while your mom is on the phone, it makes it hard for her to hear the other person.

- You're a Thinking of Others person when you keep your voice quiet in the classroom so others can concentrate on what they're doing. You're also a Thinking of Others person when you make sure your body and things aren't spilling over into other people's space. When you use a loud voice while others are trying to work, you're being a Just Me person. You're also being a Just Me person when your body or things bump into other people again and again.

When it's time to clean up at home, at school, or other places, you're a Thinking of Others person when you help out, or cooperate. This will help get the job done faster. When a job gets done faster, everyone is usually happy because they can move on to the next thing. When you don't help out, you're being a Just Me person.

It's expected behavior to be a Thinking of Others person even when no one is talking to you.

KEEP IN MIND:

When you insist your idea is best, and won't consider others' ideas, you're being a JUST Me person.

When you work in a group, you're a Thinking of Others person when you listen to other people's ideas and accept them. You do this even when it's not your favorite idea or first choice. This is also called being a flexible thinker. When you accept the ideas of others, and when you're flexible, others usually feel good. When you insist on your idea and only your idea, you're being a Just Me person.

Being a Thinking of Others person also means that even when you're doing your own thing around others, you're still thinking about the people around you. Here are some examples of being a Thinking of Others person:

- You think about how much noise you're making. For instance, you can't play a video game too loudly if your sister is doing her homework in the next room.

- You think about how long you're taking to do something. For example, you may be using the computer, but you know your sister wants a turn too.

- You think about how you leave a space after you've used it. For example, if you leave your things spilling off your desk at school, this can make the person who sees the mess frustrated. Or, if you leave a mess in your kitchen at home, other members of your family may feel bothered. A Thinking of Others person usually tries to clean up after himself when he leaves a room. That way no one has to look at his dirty dishes or trip over his things. When you leave your stuff in places it doesn't belong or leave a mess behind without cleaning up, you're being a Just Me person.

It's important to be a Thinking of Others person even at home.

Sometimes it's easy to be a Thinking of Others person and sometimes it's hard, depending on the situation. We all make mistakes at times and we learn as we go.

At times we can get stuck on one idea and we don't want to change it. Maybe it's something we really, really want to do. Or we might think our own idea or plan is better than that of others. This type of thinking can cause us to be a Just Me.

KEEP IN MIND:

Sometimes it's hard to be a Thinking of Others person.

Being a Just Me person can make others feel uncomfortable, angry, or annoyed.

Those who do a good job being Thinking of Others kids are thought of as being friendlier. In fact, being a Thinking of Others person is one thing that can help you make and keep friends. People will feel calm and possibly happy when they're around you because you're showing you're thinking about them!

This type of thinking is what we call "being friendly"! Being friendly means we're using our flexible thinking!

Thinking of OThers kids are ThoughT of as being friendLy.

When everyone is a Thinking of Others person, people feel good being together.

Now, go explore how all this information applies to you in the Thinksheets book.

LeT's Recap ChapTer 8
Thinking of Others Versus Just Me

- I'll try to remember how important it is to be a Thinking of Others person. This means I'm being cooperative and I'm thinking about others and how my behavior may make them think and feel.

- When I think about others I'm flexible and adjust my behavior based on what I know makes others feel more comfortable.

- When I'm a Thinking of Others person, people around me tend to feel good and are more likely to have good thoughts about me. When people have good thoughts about me, they'll probably want to be around me more! This will make me feel good too.

- It can sometimes be okay to be a Just Me person when no one else is around. But when I'm around other people, and I act like a Just Me, that's unexpected! People may think I am selfish because I'm doing things that show them I don't consider their thoughts or feelings or what makes them feel calm.

CHAPTER 9

How Big Is My Problem?
Size of My Problem, Part 1

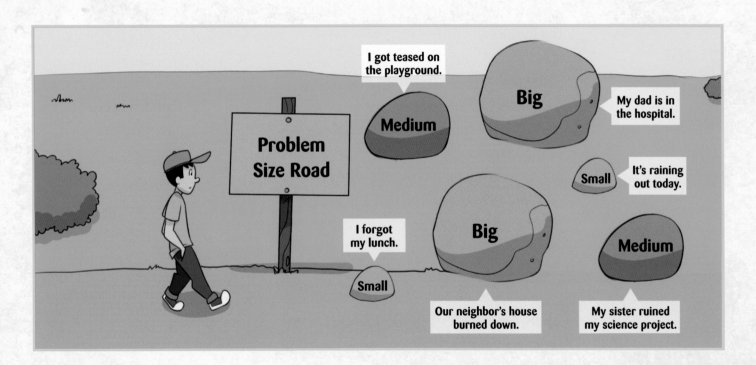

So far in this book we've talked a lot about ways you can become a better social thinker. You've worked through some thinksheets and learned strategies to help you become better at solving social problems.

But, we can't avoid problems even if we use our social brains to the best of our abilities. Problems are still bound to happen. So in this chapter (and the next one) let's talk about ways to think about problems when they occur and how to handle them in a better way. Read on!

Problems are things that happen to us that cause us to start to feel sad, or nervous, or maybe even really upset or angry. Problems come in all different sizes, just like our feelings.

KEEP IN MIND:

ProbLems come in aLL differenT siZes, jusT Like our feeLings.

Some problems are **big problems**, like an earthquake, a flood, or a tornado. A problem is also big if it causes people we care about, or sometimes even ourselves, to become hurt or sick. **Big problems may affect a lot of people.** For example, a problem is big if people can't make money for a while or they lose their place to live.

Big problems are serious problems that adults handle. They're too big for kids to figure out what to do. Big problems can make us feel nervous or sad. We might cry and see other people crying about big problems. It's okay to feel sad or scared sometimes.

Some problems are **medium problems**. **Medium problems are things that happen that we didn't expect and aren't easy to quickly fix.** Medium problems may include fighting with another person or losing something important to you. Another medium problem can be someone saying something really mean to another person or to you. **Medium problems will make you or someone around you upset.**

Very often you may have to work with a teacher or your parent to figure out how you can fix a medium problem. Here's something to remember. **Adults expect children to help solve medium problems.** They're not too big for children to handle. But it may take a little bit of time for a child to not be upset about the problem.

AduLTS expecT
chiLdren
To heLp SoLve
medium probLems.

A medium problem may affect a few people and usually takes a little bit of time to fix. For example, let's say one of your classmates keeps doing something that interrupts the class and makes it hard for you to hear your teacher. Interrupting the class or shouting out answers when the teacher doesn't want you to is unexpected behavior. The teacher probably will need to help the child change his behavior. But that student will also have to work at becoming a better member of the group.

Here's another example of a medium problem. Imagine you're waiting in line to go into school one morning. You notice one student bump into another student pretty hard. Then, both students start yelling at each other and they seem really mad. Other kids back away, which is body language that means they might be nervous about what's happening. A grown-up approaches the group and tells the two students to move apart. Once everyone has calmed down, the students talk about what happened with the help of a teacher.

KEEP IN MIND:

SmaLL probLems,

aLso caLLed gLiTches,

don'T LasT very Long

and are

"no big deaL."

Some problems are **SmaLL probLems.** They're little unexpected situations that can be easily fixed as long as you stay calm. **A small problem usually doesn't last too long.** For example, you may get upset because you don't get to play the game you want to play or you forget part of your lunch at home. **Small problems can involve just yourself, or sometimes they involve one or a few other people.**

Another name for a small problem is a **glitch**, and this means the problem is "no big deal." It's good to remember that glitches can usually be fixed easily. Sometimes you may need some help to do this from your teacher or parent or even a friend.

I think you can take care of these on your own. I'm here to help if you need me.

SomeTimes our feeLings abouT a probLem are much bigger Than The probLem iTseLf. This is something really, really important to think about. For instance, if you scream and cry because you can't play the game you prefer, you're acting like it's a medium problem. People then think your reaction is odd or unexpected and they may get upset as well. Everyone feels better when we stop to think and realize it's a small problem before reacting. This also helps the small problem get solved more quickly. That's because it's easier to think of a solution when we're calm. People will have good thoughts about us when we stay calm.

Did you know that glitches happen a lot to everyone, a lot of the time? In fact, most people expect glitches to happen at some point in their day.

If you want to figure out whether a problem is a small one, here are some questions you can ask yourself:

1. Does this problem affect many people? You can tell by noticing if other people are also upset.

2. Will this problem still exist tomorrow or the next day?

3. Does an adult need to fix this problem or help fix it?

If you answered no to at least two of these questions, your problem is probably a small problem or a glitch.

Now, go explore how all this information applies to you in the Thinksheets book.

Let's Recap Chapter 9
How Big Is My Problem?

- Problems come in all different sizes.

- I'll try to remember to think about the size of my problem and stay calm when I have a glitch. When I do that others will have good thoughts about me. If I get really upset over a glitch, it can grow in size. My big reaction will upset other people too. This is unexpected behavior and not what I want.

- A BIG problem is one that causes people we care about to become hurt or sick. Or they can't make money for a while or they lose their place to live. Big problems are serious problems that adults are in charge of. They're too big for kids to figure out what to do.

- A MEDIUM problem is one that we didn't expect and isn't easy to quickly fix. Medium problems will make you or someone around you upset. Adults expect kids to help solve medium problems. But it may take a little bit of time for a kid to not be upset about the problem.

- A SMALL problem, or a GLITCH, is a little unexpected problem that can be easily fixed. If you stay calm, stop to think about its size, and remember small problems are really no big deal, glitches can go away pretty quickly. Often glitches just affect you or maybe one other person.

CHAPTER 10

Thinking About My Reaction Size
Size of My Problem, Part 2

You've learned that problems come in different sizes. There are big problems, medium problems, and small problems, also called glitches. Now let's talk about the reactions we have to problems of different sizes.

KEEP IN MIND:

We use our social Thinking To help us match our reaction size To The size of The problem.

Our reactions are the behaviors we show on the outside that come from the feelings we have on the inside. That means we react to all sorts of things. We react to things that are good as well as our problems! We show our feelings to others through our facial expressions, gestures, sounds, and/or our words and how we say them.

Just Like problems vary in size, so do our feelings and reactions To Them.

Sometimes our feelings are the same size as the problem we're involved in. For instance, we have a big reaction and a big feeling about a big problem. Sometimes our feelings (reactions) aren't matched to the size of the problem. This can be when we get really upset (big reaction) over a small problem. It can also be when we have a small reaction to a big problem.

Here's something very important to learn. We use our social thinking to help us match our reaction size to the problem. We can think with our eyes to figure out whether our reaction size is expected or unexpected in a situation.

IT's expected That your reaction size should match The size of your problem. This is also a hidden ruLe.

When your reaction matches the size of your problem, people around you are more understanding of your behavior. They'll have okay thoughts about you.

Your reaction size should match the size of your problem.

But when your reaction size is bigger than the size of your problem, people may feel worried, annoyed, nervous or stressed. They'll have uncomfortable thoughts about you. Plus, when people around you feel stressed by your behavior, this creates a whole new problem!

Your feelings and your reactions happen together most of the time. But they're separate things to think about and work on. It's always okay to *feel* upset or disappointed if that's what you feel. **Each of us has our own feelings. But what we really have to think about is what we *do* with those feelings.** We need to think about the reactions we show to others.

Here are some examples of problems and reaction sizes to read and think about:

EMERGENCY! This is a bad accident. Can someone call an ambulance!

A big reaction to a big problem.

- A car accident can often be a big problem. Most people agree it could be expected behavior to become very upset, cry out loud, or yell that there's an emergency. Yelling and crying out loud are big reactions. These would be expected when you're in the middle of a big problem.

- If you lose your book report on the day the class is supposed to turn it in, this would be a medium problem. Expected behavior might be to feel upset, almost cry, or call home for help. Feeling upset, almost crying, and getting help from an adult are medium reactions. These would be expected for a medium problem. If someone yelled or cried out loud following a medium problem, this is described as **overreacting**. Most people would feel worried or nervous and have uncomfortable thoughts about that person. Overreacting is an unexpected behavior.

- A tornado that rips houses and buildings apart is a big problem. It would be expected that people have a big reaction to a tornado. It would be unexpected for people to have a little reaction or no reaction to a tornado.

A medium reaction to a medium problem.

Overreacting to a medium problem.

KEEP IN MIND:

IT's always okay To feel what you feel. BUT iT's expected ThaT we all continue To learn To control how we react To our feelings.

When you don't get to play what you want to play, this is a glitch. **It's expected that small reactions go with small problems.** People expect that you might possibly share your opinion out loud. You might say something like "I really wanted to play baseball instead of soccer." But they would expect you to calm your upset feelings and play anyway. Or, when someone loses a game, people would understand if that person feels disappointed. The expected behavior would be to say something like, "Oh well... maybe we can play again." This is having a small reaction.

We have to practice making our reactions match the size of a problem and the more we practice, the easier it gets. One strategy is to pause and think with our eyes when we have a problem. We use our social thinking to figure out if our reaction matches the problem. If it does, we're okay. If it doesn't, we can change our behavior. This is called **"adjusting our reaction."** When kids are learning to control their feelings, we might see them have a

A small reaction to a small problem.

medium reaction like crying. And then they stop and think and change their reaction and make it small. For example, they might cry for few seconds, take a breath, and then say, "no big deal" or keep playing. When grown-ups see kids change their reaction in this way, they know the kids are thinking about their reaction size. The adults know kids have to learn to be better social thinkers. When people quickly change their medium or big reactions to small problems and make them small reactions, we call this "letting it go." Or we can call it "making a quick recovery."

A big reaction to a small problem.

We all have to learn to let a problem go when it's only a glitch. This means we stop thinking about it and stop acting *really* upset. We all have to stop sometimes and think about how our reaction matches up to the problem. If we're overreacting, we then need to calm down and try to make a better choice in behavior. This helps keep other people comfortable and wanting to help you!

When we overreact we need to calm down and try to make a better choice.

Now, go explore how all this information applies to you in the Thinksheets book.

LeT's Recap Chapter 10
Thinking About My Reaction Size

🔵 I'll start to think about the size of my problems and remember that my reaction size should match the size of my problem. That's expected!

🔵 It's always okay to feel how I feel, but I really need to think about what behaviors I show to others. When I react to my problem in a way that makes sense to others, they feel more comfortable about my behavior.

🔵 When my reaction size is bigger than the size of my problem, that's unexpected. Others may be stressed by my behavior. This creates a whole new problem for me!

🔵 My parents and teachers will help me figure out how to match my reactions to the size of the problem.

🔵 When I know it's a small problem, I'll take deep breaths to try and relax. I'll try to remind myself that my problem is a small one so it's no big deal.

CHAPTER 11

Doing An Activity or Just Hanging Out

Doing a fun activity or hanging out together is something most of us like to do. Although people don't usually talk about it, how we use our time together can affect how much we enjoy being together.

KEEP IN MIND:

Set up and clean up

should go quickly

so we have more

time for the

activity.

Our time together can be divided into three parts: set up, play/hang out, and clean up. It's expected that all people join in all three parts. Doing the activity or hanging out should take the most time! Set up and clean up should take far less time so everyone feels good about the experience.

The first part of an activity is Set Up. During set up we figure out what we want to do together. We listen to all ideas and then pick one. It also means we get things we need to play the game or do the activity. For instance, before we can play a game like softball, we need to get our materials or bodies ready for the game. It may also mean we have to agree on the rules of our game or decide who will go first. Set up usually only takes a few minutes.

For a board game, set up means a few things. We open the box, take out the board, choose which game piece we want to use, etc. We also stay calm and use our flexible thinking if we don't get the game piece we want! We want to be a Thinking of Others person, not a Just Me person!

For soccer, set up means deciding who will be on which team and deciding together which team will use which goal.

When playing a game together on a tablet, set up means deciding which app to use, who will go first, and even thinking about how often to pass the tablet back and forth to take turns.

Even if we just want to hang out together, there are still some things to figure out, like where to hang out, for how long, and maybe whether or not people are hungry and want some snacks to munch on!

When everyone works together as a group, set up goes quickly!

The second part of an activity is when we actually do The acTiViTy. This is what most people think of when someone says "let's play" or "let's hang out."

This is where we play the game, take turns, move our bodies, think together, and
— depending on the game — win or lose. Or it's the time we spend together
watching television, looking at YouTube videos, going to the mall or a movie, or just
talking. This is often the fun part and where kids usually want to spend most of their
time. It can also be the disappointing part when you're not having good luck during
a game, or you wanted to do something different than the rest of the
group. Even in that situation you can feel glad that you're
included with others in the group.

When set up is quick, there's more time for fun!

The third and last part of an activity is **CLean Up**. It's probably the least interesting part of being together, but it's important. Why? It's because clean up brings the activity to a close in an expected way and everyone feels okay about it. This usually takes just a few minutes as well.

Clean up is quick when everyone helps out.

When playing a card game or a board game, clean up means first putting the board, cards, and pieces neatly in their box. Then we finish by putting the cover on the box, and placing the box back on a shelf or in a closet.

For tag, soccer, basketball, baseball, or any other game that involves moving your body, clean up usually happens in a similar way once it's decided the game is over. If this is a game played during the school day, kids might need to put equipment away and clean up by forming a line to go back inside.

For a classroom activity such as an art or a science project, clean up means putting all the art supplies or materials away, and throwing away or putting in the recycling bin the materials that won't be used again. We also might need to make sure materials are organized as we put them away. This is so it's easy to pick up where we left off if we want to finish our group project later.

> CLean up brings The activity To a cLose in a way ThaT heLps everyone feeL okay abouT The Time They spenT TogeTher.

When we're just hanging out together, clean up means we figure out what we need to do as our time together ends. For instance, we may need to pick up any food, snacks, or materials we've been sharing, say our good-byes and maybe talk about the next time to get together. It would be unexpected for someone in the group to skip clean up and just leave without saying anything to the others.

Sometimes we only have a certain amount of time for an activity, and usually kids want to spend most of their time doing the activity itself. So, it's important to work together to do set up and clean up quickly and carefully. When kids work cooperatively together in these ways, there's usually more time to enjoy the fun part. For example, imagine you have 30 minutes to do the three parts of the activity. That might mean you use about five minutes to set up, five minutes to clean up, which leaves you 20 minutes for the activity. When there's more time for fun, everyone feels happy and has good thoughts about each other.

Here are some examples of set up and clean up taking too long. When these things happen, some kids may feel annoyed, frustrated, or impatient. As a result they may not want to do something again with the same group or people in the group.

**SeT up migHT Take Too Long** when any of these things happens:

- Kids can't agree on the rules of the game.

- Everyone wants to go first.

- Someone throws the cards when dealing them instead of nicely passing them. Players have to stop and pick their cards up off the ground.

- One person in the group doesn't help and lets everyone else do all the work while setting up the activity.

- Kids argue over what color game piece they want or who gets to hold the tablet.

- The students in the classroom can't decide what to do together. No one will compromise.

ALL Three parts of an activity need To be done To work, play, or hang ouT successfully with oThers.

Clean up might Take Too Long when:

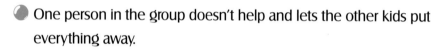

- One person in the group doesn't help and lets the other kids put everything away.

- Someone throws things in the box, and they bounce out again or break.

- Someone tosses a game back on its shelf, it falls off, and pieces go everywhere.

- One person gets really, really upset that she can't keep playing. Now that person — and everyone else — has a big problem!

- One person is really really slow getting his coat and backpack together so they can leave. Everyone else is waiting on him.

The important thing to remember with the three parts of an activity is that ALL THREE parts need to be accomplished to work, play, or hang out successfully with others.

When you join in the three parts of an activity/hanging out, others will feel okay and relaxed. They'll have okay thoughts about you and enjoy being around you. That means you'll probably have more fun too. It's important to help out and think about what you're doing during set up and clean up so the people you're with see you as a Thinking of Others person and that you're not "wasting other people's time."

It's expected that everyone help with clean up.

Now, go explore how all this information applies to you in the Thinksheets book.

LeT's Recap ChapTer 11
Doing An Activity or Just Hanging Out

- I'll try to remember that there are always three parts of an activity or hanging out:

  1. Set up

  2. Doing the activity or the time spent hanging out

  3. Clean up

- All activities take time. It's expected that I participate or help out in each part of the activity and stay aware of moving through set up and clean up quickly and efficiently. I know that when I use my flexible thinking to move quickly through set up and I help out during clean up, we all have more time to do the activity or hang out together.

- I can move quickly through set up by being flexible as our group makes decisions.

- I can help out best during clean up by listening to others and treating materials with care as I put them away.

- Kids prefer to do an activity or hang out with kids who join in all three parts of an activity.

- These same ideas apply when I'm just hanging out with others. I still need to think about others and what they want to do or talk about and how to make our time together enjoyable.

Glossary

Big problem: A problem is big if it causes people we care about or ourselves to become hurt or sick. It's also big if people can't make money for a while or they lose their place to live. Some examples are an earthquake, a flood, or a tornado. Big problems are serious problems that adults handle. They're too big for children to figure out what to do. Big problems can make us feel nervous or sad. We may cry and see other people crying about big problems. (See also Medium problem and Glitch.)

Body in the group: When people turn or move their bodies to show others they want to be with each other, we describe this as their "body is in the group." This may mean we face each other when we speak or we move closer to another person. It may even mean we stay together when walking or moving to a new space. Our body is in the group when our head, eyes, shoulders, trunk, legs, and feet are pointing toward the person speaking or the group and we are in close proximity to others.

Brain in the group: Keeping your brain in the group means you try to keep your thoughts focused on what other people are talking about.

Clean up: (see the Three Parts of doing an activity/hanging out)

Expected behavior: Behavior that most people do in a certain place or certain situation that follows the rules for that situation. Some of those rules may be hidden rules that people need to figure out. When people have expected behavior, others usually have good or okay thoughts about that person. (Read about the opposite: unexpected behavior.)

Flexible thinking: When we think in new or different ways about a situation, and when we feel okay with others thinking different things than we do.

Glitch: A small problem, a little unexpected situation that can be easily fixed as long as you stay calm. A small problem usually doesn't last too long. Glitches can involve just yourself or sometimes they involve one or a few other people too. They can usually be fixed easily, even though sometimes you may need some help to do this from your teacher or parent or even a friend.

Good thoughts/Uncomfortable thoughts: We all have thoughts about others. When another person makes us feel good, we probably have good thoughts about that person. For example, we may think, "He's nice" or "I like her." We usually have good thoughts about others when they act in an expected way for a situation. When another person makes us feel not so good, or upset, we may have uncomfortable thoughts about him or her. These are some examples of uncomfortable thoughts: "I don't like when she does that," "I feel nervous because of what he's doing," or "I'm upset at her for doing that." Uncomfortable thoughts usually happen when someone is using unexpected behavior.

Group: A group is more than one person sharing the same space or interacting together in a situation. A group can be as small as two people or it can be large, with many people.

Group plan: When people are together they usually are thinking about and doing the same thing. This is called the group plan. Following the group plan is different than following one's own plan.

Hidden rules: Most situations have hidden rules in them, which are the ways that people should behave in that situation that aren't said out loud or taught to us directly. People don't usually tell others the hidden rules for every situation. But, people are expected to figure them out by thinking with their eyes and listening with their ears to the people around them.

Just Me person: Someone who thinks only about himself or herself. It's okay to be a Just Me when it's a time that you can do what you want to do and it won't disrupt others.

Medium problem: Things that happen that we didn't expect and aren't easy to quickly fix. Medium problems may include fighting with another person, losing something important to you, or someone saying something really mean to another person or to you. Medium problems will make you or someone around you upset. Adults and kids usually solve medium problems together.

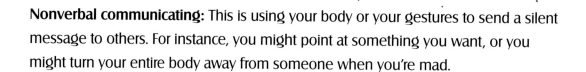

Nonverbal communicating: This is using your body or your gestures to send a silent message to others. For instance, you might point at something you want, or you might turn your entire body away from someone when you're mad.

Observing: Taking your time to look around at the people and the situation to find helpful clues about what's going on. Observing involves using your eyes, ears, and other senses, and thinking with your eyes.

People files: As we gather information about other people and situations, we keep that information in our brain in an imaginary set of files that we call our People Files. Everyone has their own set of people files in their brains and they can be different from person to person.

Problem: Something that happens that was not part of the plan and causes us to feel sad, nervous, upset, angry, or have other negative feelings.

Reactions: Our reactions are the behaviors we show on the outside that come from the feelings we have on the inside.

Reaction size: We all have reactions to problems, and our reactions usually have feelings attached to them. It's expected behavior (and a hidden rule) that your reaction should only be as big as your problem. This means you can have a big reaction to a big problem, a medium reaction to a medium problem, and a small reaction to a glitch. When your reaction matches the size of your problem, other people are more understanding of your behavior.

Set up: (see the Three Parts of doing an activity/hanging out)

Situation: A big word that means all the things around you. When you're using social thinking in a situation, you have to think about the *what*, the *who*, and the *where*. This means you think about what's happening, where it's happening, and who is involved in what's happening.

Small problem: (see Glitch)

Smart guess: When you use what you already know and any clues you can find in the situation you're in, you make what's called a smart guess. (Read about the opposite: Wacky guess.)

Social detective: When people are good observers, they start to act like social detectives. That's because they're figuring out what people are thinking and feeling around them.

Social memory: This is using our brain to store all the facts and details that we've learned about people and situations. We can use our social memory to figure out what to say to others and what to do in a situation by remembering what we know about them.

Social thinking: The type of thinking your brain does about yourself and other people in relation to each other. When you use your social thinking, you think about what others are trying to do or tell you and what you can do to let people know what you want or how you feel.

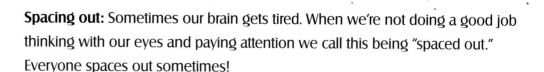

Spacing out: Sometimes our brain gets tired. When we're not doing a good job thinking with our eyes and paying attention we call this being "spaced out." Everyone spaces out sometimes!

Stuck thinking: Stuck on your own ideas; thinking about only one thing or thinking in only one way. This is the opposite of flexible thinking and is unexpected behavior. When you show stuck thinking, situations are more difficult and people can feel tense, frustrated, sad or mad.

Thinking and feeling: What we think always affects how we feel. Feelings are physical sensations in our bodies that seem to pop up on their own. Really, they're related to a thought we've had. Most of the time, we act in a certain way or do a certain thing because of how we're thinking or feeling.

Thinking of Others person: A Thinking of Others person means you think about how your behavior makes others think and feel. When you're a Thinking of Others person, you're always thinking about the other people who are sharing space with you or may be coming to share your space very soon. (Read about the opposite: a Just Me person.)

Thinking with your eyes: In Social Thinking we call the ability to observe and make sense of what's in front of us thinking with your eyes. It pretty much means what it sounds like. You use your eyes to look at people and things, and then you use your brain to think about what you're seeing. This helps you figure out if you should be involved in what's going on. If you're supposed to be involved, what should you do? You think with your eyes more and figure it out!

Three Parts of doing an activity/hanging out: (1) **Set up** is getting our materials or bodies ready for a game, an activity, or just spending time with others; (2) **Doing an activity/hanging out** is the time we spend involved in the activity; (3) **Clean up** is ending the game or activity by putting away our materials or deciding together that it's time to end what we're doing.

Unexpected behavior: The opposite of expected behavior. It's behavior that most people wouldn't do in a situation and isn't expected. Unexpected behavior is when people aren't following the expected rules, hidden or stated, in the situation. When people have unexpected behavior, others usually have uncomfortable thoughts about that person.

Wacky guess: This is a silly guess you make when you don't have any information about the situation and can't find any clues to help you think about what's going on.

Whopping topic change: Making comments or asking questions about things that are completely unrelated to what the group is talking about or doing. This is unexpected behavior that makes people uncomfortable.